An Ear to the Ground

An Ear to the Ground

A Wireless Operator's War with Bomber Command

Warrant Officer Frank Bell

with

Joan and Ken Bell

An imprint of
MENTION THE WAR PUBLICATIONS

First published in the United Kingdom in 2017 by Bomber Command Books, an imprint of Mention the War Ltd. Leeds LS28 5HA, England.

Copyright 2017 © Joan and Ken Bell

Cover design: Topics – The Creative Partnership www.topicdesign.co.uk
Cover image: Geoff Hill.

A CIP catalogue reference for this book is available from the British Library

ISBN 978-1-911255-27-7

Other titles about 514 Squadron RAF from Bomber Command Books

Nothing Can Stop Us – The Definitive History of 514 Squadron RAF
- Simon Hepworth, Andrew Porrelli and Harry Dison.

Striking Through Clouds – The War Diary of 514 Squadron RAF
- Simon Hepworth and Andrew Porrelli.

Lancasters at Waterbeach - Some of the Story of 514 Squadron
- Harry Dison

Skid Row to Buckingham Palace
- Ed Greenburgh

The Boy and the Bomber
- Francois Ydier

…and in the morning… The Casualty Records of 514 Squadron
- Barry Hope

These books, and others relating to RAF Bomber Command, are available from Amazon worldwide or from our website, www.bombercommandbooks.com

Contents

Top: The 514 Squadron crest was approved by King George VI. The sword piercing a cloud symbolises the unit's pioneering work with the GH blind bombing system. Above: The memorial in St. John the Baptist's church, Waterbeach, to the 437 air and ground crew who lost their lives while serving with 514 Squadron.

11

Preface

I would just like to say a big thank you to our mother, Joan Bell, for transcribing our father's notes of his time as a wireless operator in the RAF during the Second World War. Thanks also to Simon Hepworth for all his help and support in the publication of this book and to Geoff Lee for allowing us to use his wonderful painting for the cover.

Kenneth and Andrew Bell

Frank Bell, 29th November 1924 – 12th June 2016. Frank was 21 years old when this photo was taken.

Prologue

Frank Bell was born and lived in Darlington all his life. As a 17-year-old he and his friend would leave home about 6pm and cycle to Middleton–St–George to watch the Whitley bombers landing and taking off, returning home at 8.30 pm. He joined the Air Training Corps to learn everything he could about the RAF. He was fortunate to go to camp at RAF Topcliffe and was lucky to fly for 20 minutes in a Halifax. He knew for certain all he wanted to do was fly.

On returning from camp, with his Grandfathers permission he went to Middlesbrough and volunteered for the RAF. His application was successful. All he had to do was wait for his 18th birthday. He continued to attend ATC twice a week concentrating on Morse Code. Two weeks before his birthday he received his notification. He was called up for military service in the RAF. He kept diaries and later transcribed these with his memories into copious notes. His crew flew 40 operations and survived. His story is a personal one full of descriptions of the raids, the near squeaks, the hazards, the sadness of losing friends and many nuggets of information not usually mentioned. It is also a compelling account of the meticulous planning that went into the planning of the raids, and gives a detailed insight into the life of Wireless Operator in a heavy bomber in the Second World War.

Decisions and Ambitions

A lot of water (and time) has passed under the bridge since I last flew on operations in the RAF and sometimes you wonder was it worthwhile. Remembering old pals and friends you made in all the various courses you had to go through Training Command. You had to reach proficiency and to have confidence in yourself and in your crew before going to a squadron and on to operations. Quite a lot were killed in accidents in Training Command, never even reaching an operational station or squadron. But the loss of these young (and they were mainly young lives) were allowed for in statistics of the 'higher ups' in the air ministry, and of Bomber Command itself. They were allowed for in a dispensable quota of losses in the whole of Flying Training Command. Ironical that even as on operational flying, Lady Luck played her part in flying training.

Time may try and dim your memory and on certain things it does but having been through something like this most of it IS remembered. Although I was very young when I volunteered for aircrew, and I suppose, daft, impetuous, and sort of patriotic, looking for excitement and also for a meaning in life, it is something I am glad I did not miss doing even though, with hindsight, our chances of getting through a tour in Bomber Command were never good. Since those days I have given thanks many a time for having survived, and sometimes on thinking back I get goose pimples on my neck when I remember the escapes and narrow squeaks we had. I thank God for the type of crew we were. We had confidence in each other knowing each one of us was as proficient as it was possible to be. A crew who had faith in each other and so were confident and content. All we needed was for Lady Luck to be flying with us and she was.

How did it all start? I'll tell you.

I can remember it as if it were yesterday, cycling along the country roads from Darlington to the RAF station at Middleton–St-George, there to spend a pleasant evening with a friend of mine, just watching the Whitley bombers landing and taking off. To me they looked like flying coffins as they flew along nose down tail up. We used to leave home about 6pm, spend a couple of hours there and cycle home about 8.30pm. I can remember it was April or May in 1940, or was it 1941? No matter. I loved to cycle out there and watch them, wishing it would be me flying them. I am sure that was what started it all, forming my ambition to fly. Eventually in August 1941, I joined the Air Training Corp and proceeded to take in and learn everything and anything that would help me to enter the RAF when I came of age at 18.

In the last week of May 1942, I was fortunate enough to go with the ATC for a week's camp at RAF Topcliffe and thoroughly enjoyed it. Now, though I didn't understand and realise at the time this was an operational squadron. However, they also flew practice and local flights, so I was hoping against hope I might get lucky and get a trip up and I remember one afternoon I WAS lucky. There was an aircraft going up on a short flying test (NFT) and I asked the pilot if there was any chance of a fly up and he said OK. I was over the moon. I had no parachute. Still what the heck! The aircraft was a four engine Halifax and consequently flying without helmet and earphones the noise was terrific. The noise of the four engines and the resulting vibration was overwhelming and yet it gave you a sense of the power available. Having to keep out of the way of the crew in their duties I only managed to get an occasional glimpse of the outside world, but it was exciting, and I enjoyed it. At last I had flown and though it seemed to be over quite quickly we had actually been airborne 20 minutes. When we came in to land it was like a slow sinking sensation and my ears started to tickle and plop. I knew now that was what I wanted to do. Join the RAF and fly but I was only 17 years old.

As my grandfather had brought me up I talked it over with him when I arrived back from camp and after mulling it over for a while he said if that is what you want to do it was alright with him.

So off I went to the RAF recruiting Office at Middlesbrough and volunteered for the RAF. That was July 1942. I was given a medical and an aptitude test to see what in their eyes I would be best qualified to train for. I had said I wanted to go as aircrew and as a pilot if possible. But I was told that at present time they were not after air crew and my best bet was to go in as ground crew and train as a wireless operator and then, if while on that course air crew volunteers were asked for to apply for aircrew training then (WOP/AG). So I agreed to do just that. All I had to do now was to wait until my 18th birthday on 29th November 1942.

Incidentally I was told that when I was called up I would have to have another RAF medical. Also, if and when I was remustered for aircrew I would have to have an intelligence exam, go before an aircrew selection board and also have a stiff aircrew medical.

I continued going to the ATC two nights a week learning all I could. I concentrated learning the Morse Code knowing it would be a great help and advantageous to me when I did go into the RAF. I was keen, young and daft. I spent a lot of time doing aircraft recognition both English, German and Italian from various angles. Some aircraft were easy to identify but others were very difficult. There would usually be only one slight difference between two similar looking, but entirely different types of aircraft. The important thing was identification would sometimes have to be made very quickly, and positively. Lives would depend on it. Action occurs very fast in the air. You would most probably have only a second's glance at it and a decision would have to be made and acted on smartly as to whether it was friendly or an enemy.

In the ATC we learned to march and salute properly and also quite a lot of information about the general running of the RAF.

I was growing impatient wanting to get in the RAF and the time passed. Two weeks before my 18th birthday I received an envelope stamped DHMS. Notification I was being called up for military service in the RAF. I was to report to RAF recruitment Centre at Padgate as early as possible on Monday morning 30th November 1942, ration coupons, clothes coupons, gas mask and an empty suitcase. The empty suitcase was for my civilian clothes to be sent home.

The Sunday night of my birthday couldn't come quick enough. It was going to be the start of a big new adventure. I can remember leaving home that Sunday evening about 10pm to catch the train to York changing there for the train to Manchester, then change stations for the train to Padgate.

There were quite a few other chaps waiting outside the station. A corporal was there getting everyone organised. On arriving at Padgate we were taken immediately to the ablutions for a shave and wash and brush up, then to the dining hall for a much welcome breakfast. Breakfast over things became a bit hectic. We were lined up and marched to the station sick quarters where we underwent a full medical and passed free from infection. One man failed and was dismissed. We were then marched over to another building and sworn in. We were now definitely in the RAF. Next we were hustled round to the stores building, kitted out and detailed to the billet we were to live in. The billets were long wooden huts accommodating 20 men. Each had a steel sprung bed with three square, biscuit type mattress and four rough blankets – no sheets, plus one flat pillow and boy, did it take some getting used to. One slim locker held our clothes and equipment.

Then started the drill, discipline, lectures, physical training and worst of all we had from time to time go to the coal dump and fill cwt sacks with coal. We ended up black with coal dust. We were not allowed to leave camp, so we played snooker or cards at the NAAFI or went to the camp cinema.

On Thursday, four days after arriving, at 7pm the corporal marched in and told us to get our kit together we were leaving that night. We hadn't a clue what was happening. We were marched to the station where an empty train was waiting. We had no idea where we were going and guess where the train stopped –Blackpool and this was where we were going to do our square bashing and our initial training in the middle of winter. All the hotels and guesthouses had been commandeered for the duration of the war. We were allocated our billet. I was at 72 Palatine

Road with five others. We then had lectures in a vast hall in Victoria Street. The following day we were marched to the Methodist Church hall in Dickson Road for our jabs. It was decked out as the medical centre. We were given the weekend to recover. We were so ill with swollen arms we could do nothing.

Life became routine with drill and guard duty but every afternoon from 1pm-4.45pm was Morse code, held in the Winter Garden Complex. There were long tables in the downstairs section seating ten each side with an instructor at the head sending the Morse. You put on your headset picked up your pencil and wrote on the paper ALL afternoon. It was boring but necessary to get speed up to 12 words per minute. If you failed the test at the end of the course you were thrown off the course as a wireless operator.

During the course a day was set aside for a special event. It was a forced march along the promenade and coast road to Rossall near Fleetwood to the firing range with full pack. We had a three-hour session with rifles and Sten gun then marched back to our digs knackered. The weeks passed, and the Morse code speed was upped. More men fell by the wayside. Those who passed the final test were issued with a ration card and travel warrants and sent on seven days leave after which we had to travel down to Hereford and thence by RAF transport to No. 4 Radio School, Madley.

Air Crew Cadets — No. 4 Radio School
MADLEY

ENTRY No. 37

Madley

Madley was a very spread out camp about 6 miles from Hereford along the Hay-on-Wye road set in lovely countryside with apple orchards and cider making.

There were two parts to the camp ground wireless operators and aircrew wireless operators plus three hangers, two runways which could be used in either direction in relation to the whims of the wind. The aircraft used were twin engine de Havilland Rapide that could take up six personnel. Also, the single engine Percival Proctor aircraft that could accommodate two men; pilot and wireless operator. These were used at an advanced stage.

At this point I was concerned with the ground wireless officer course and boy was there some foot slogging to do just walking from one unit to another. It was marching everywhere, two abreast in squads of thirty airmen.

This course was an intensification of Morse code, sending and receiving getting your speed of each up to 18 words a minute. Practical manipulation of different types of receivers and transmitters, theory of the sets and also of electrical knowledge on ohms, condensers, chokes, generators, batteries etc. and now we had to learn about Q code and X signals and general procedure for working on wireless transmitters. There was also semaphore signalling to learn. This was just for knowledge. We did learn to use the Aldis lamp for sending Morse air to air and air to ground.

It was a hard grind and an intensive course, plenty of swotting in the evening. Half way through the course we got a long weekend break. On our return a circular was sent around they were looking for volunteers for aircrew duties. I must state here and now that flying was voluntary, and no man could be forced to fly. But woe betide if after all the expensive specialist training an individual opted out or refused to fly (this usually happened when getting near to operations or actually on a squadron) even though it might be his nerve had gone he would be classified LMF lack of moral fibre in other words having no guts –a coward. He would immediately be stripped of his rank and wings – sometimes publicly and posted away from the camp as soon as possible. Most probably the same day. Subsequently he would be given the most menial of jobs for a long time until someone at headquarters thought he had had enough and given the opportunity to remuster and train for something on the ground. It wasn't guaranteed and the stigma of LMF would be on his records for good.

I volunteered for aircrew (wireless operator-air gunner and had another intelligence test, an aptitude exam also an aircrew selection board interview. Next to have a severe aircrew medical and I passed. I was now aircrew and was given a white flash to put on the front of my forage cap.

I had to continue with the course but now I was sweating. If I failed everything would be wiped out. Thankfully I passed the exams. Now I was a ground wireless operator and so I put the sparks badge on my arm.

We were kept hanging around doing nothing for another week and then the majority of the lads who were ground wireless operators were sent on leave and to report to their various new postings. I and about ten others were given 10 days leave and told to report back to Madley to do the air wireless course. One thing this time we had the luxury of sleeping between crisp white sheets and blankets. A perk of being aircrew.

This course started with lectures then on to new procedures, different types of wireless equipment, engine driven generators, how to operate a/c with old w/t sets. After gaining experience with all the old difficult sets we went on to the new Marconi sets, which were much better to operate and more powerful.

The course commenced on 26.8.43 and it was lectures at first. This time aircraft equipment to learn about, also different types of w/t procedure to take in, air to ground and air to air etc. We had to learn about different types of A/C wireless equipment, both W/T and R/T, and also auxiliary equipment such as engine driven generators etc. We had to learn to operate in A/C with the old W/T sets, such as the receiver 1082 and transmitter 1083, and the old TR9 for Radio Telephony. The 1082/1083 were terrible to use in the air. Coils to plug in and pull out every time you changed the wavelength. The coils kept falling all over the place, nothing but a damn nuisance! But when we went on to the new Marconi, receiver 1155 and transmitter T1154, they were much better to operate and much more powerful.

Then came the day for my first flight in a de Havilland Rapide (Dominie) There was the pilot, instructor and 5 of us pupils. We took turns on the wireless that was old and difficult to manage at first. We had half an hour each which was enough for the first time up and some of us were definitely queasy when we landed. Those dominies were quite light and bounced up and down a lot and later it would be worse still because the single engine Percival Proctor was lighter still. Over the next two weeks I did about thirteen trips and then progressed to the Proctors for about ten trips each lasting about 90 minutes I passed out on the course on 30th November 1943. I was promoted and officially became 1783280 Sgt Bell F. w/op aircrew. I can't remember why, but we were kept hanging around at Madley for another three weeks doing exactly nothing.

Then suddenly we were sent on seven days leave which covered Christmas Day 1943 and then we had to make our own way to no. 10 Air Gunnery School at Barrow–in-Furness. The aerodrome was actually on Walney Island. The day after we arrived we were detailed as a burial party. Three days earlier one of the Anson aircraft had crashed killing all on board. We had to attend the funerals for all seven with rifles and fixed bayonets firing three rounds in salute as the coffins were lowered. What a start!

As usual the first weeks were in the classroom on theory this included hydraulic systems and types of gun turrets, firing from fixed gun turrets, the Browning machine gun, stripping it down and assembling it in the confined space of a gun turret. We had to recognise types of bullets, their markings and the order they were assembled in the feed belts, armour piercing, ordinary and incendiary also use of.5 machine gun. It was a relief to start flying again in an Anson with a Browning in it and a Drogue towing aircraft. We took turns firing tracer bullets into the sea to get the feel of the turret and the guns. There was also instruction on a.5 machine gun.

It was a relief when we did start flying once more. The A/Cs were Anson's with a mid-upper gun turret with a Browning in it. The drogue-towing A/C was a single engine Martinet. Five pupils went up with an instructor and the first lessons were just firing tracer bullets into the sea just to get the feel of the turret and gun. The next couple of flights were called Beam Relative Spied Tracer (B.R.S.T.), when the Anson flew parallel with the drogue-towing Martinet and we had to hit the drogue. We would be flying 200 to 300 yards off and each pupil would have 300 rounds to fire off. Each pupil's bullets would have a different colour dye paint on the tips so as to identify his number of hits. If you managed to hit the Drogue 3 or 4 times out of 300 you were lucky and dubbed a 'hot shot'. The guns were so old, the bullets used rattled on the way out. Then you had the exercise that was when the Anson flew from one side to the other under the drogue firing as you crossed under. I remember once the Martinet releasing the Drogue and shooting off as fast as he could go.

When we got back there was an irate pilot waiting for us and the language was not decent! Although the Drogue on the tour was 200 feet or more behind the Martinet someone had missed the Drogue completely and there were 4 or 5 bullet holes through the Martinets tail rudder. Then there were the cine-camera exercises. Instead of firing bullets you were shooting film. What you saw on the screen from you film was what you were hitting. Some were just black sky. It was quite an enjoyable course and most days we were finished by 5pm each day.

On 25th February 1944 I passed out as an air gunner. I was now 1783280 SGT. Bell W/OP A/G. We hung around for a couple of days and then we started to get cleared from different sections on the camp prior to going on leave.

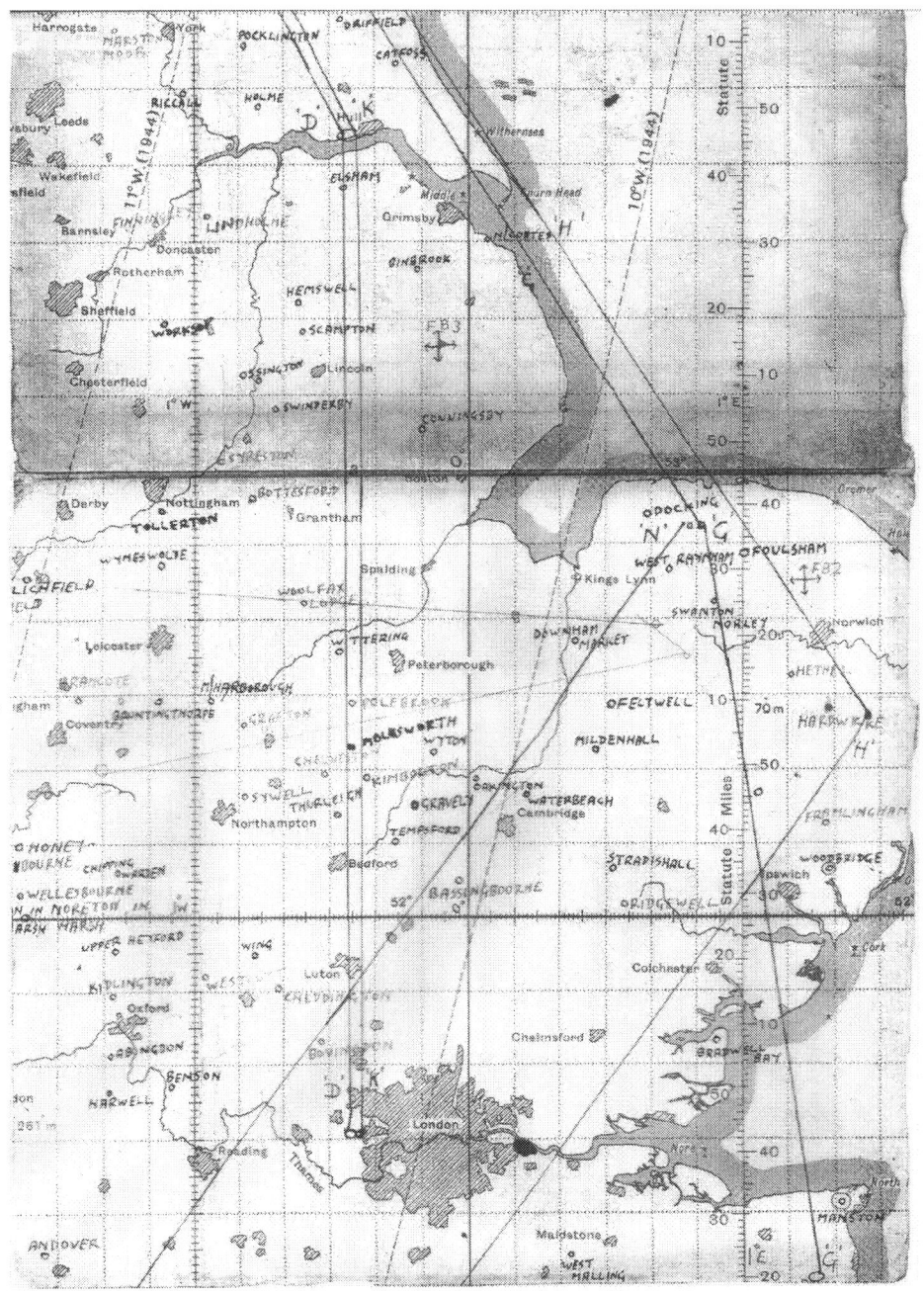

Maps showing location of airbases

27

Crewing Up

Practice, practice and more practice.

The Hendy crew at 514 Squadron, taken beside their Lancaster NN776, A2-D before the flight to Chemnitz on 14th February 1945. From left to right: F/Lt. Fred. Hendy, pilot; Sgt Taffy Harris, rear gunner, P/O Rob Simons, navigator; P/O Pat Jackson, bomb aimer; W/O George Sales, mid-upper gunner; F/Sgt Frank Bell, WOP/AG; Sgt Ernie Wall, flight engineer.

15th March 1944

I returned to Hereford. With it being so late in the day we were just booked in, given bedding and allocated a hut for the night. Formalities were completed the next morning, and we were informed that we were being held there until our posting came through. Our time was taken up with lectures and aircraft recognition. After tea we usually went into Hereford to one of the cinemas or wander round the airfield observing what was going on. One afternoon we were just laying on the grass and suddenly heard quite a new sound of a different type of aircraft coming into land and, yes, there it was, a Beaufighter. Once it got to the terminal strip we couldn't get to it quick enough. Compared to the Dragon

Rapides and Percival Proctors it looked huge and solid. There were four machine guns on its wings and two cannons protruding from its nose. Some fire power.

After two weeks' time began to drag and praying for a posting soon. It was another twelve days before it came.

10th April 1944
We were leaving the next day. Our destination was No.9 AFU at Llandwrog, North Wales. The journey on various modes of transport took an interminable time to reach Pwllheli. Three large lorries were waiting to take us over the mountains to a place called Llandwrog. It was only 15 miles but seemed much longer going up and down over the mountains. The camp and aerodrome were on the coastline. Very picturesque but in bad weather the actually encroached on the airfield, and at times the runway.

Life was comparatively easy, meaning no 'bull' or parades, just learning the job and flying –getting up to standard and better. Lots of wireless theory, wireless transmission procedure and the never-ending Morse. After 2 weeks in the classroom we commenced cross country flying. They were mainly for trainee navigators to find their way around the country and also for wireless operators to gain more experience. We had to give the navigators bearings and 'fixes or positions given by stations. Also, we had to transmit our position, height, speed and time of origin to group control every hour. This was to let them know we were still airborne and everything was ok. In all we did eleven cross country trips interspersed with lectures. The flights lasted 2 to 4 hours. The last I did was a night flight.

16th May 1944
When the course finished we weren't kept hanging around long. Three days later we were on our way to no.16 Operational Training Unit, Upper Heyford, near Oxford. It was late, so we were given bedding, allocated a hut and formalities completed next morning. We were treated to lectures from the C.O. and Signals Officer. We were then informed we would be 'crewed up' and that would be an all-day job.

Sure enough, we were assembled in a large lecture hall. Pilots, navigators, bomb aimers, gunners, wireless operators. No flight engineers. They would be picked up at our next station when we would convert to four engine aircraft. If you ever made it. I say this in all seriousness as losses at O.T.U.s were getting quite alarming.

We were addressed by the chief flying instructor who told us we had all morning to mingle and get to know each other and then form ourselves into crews. We had all day to do this, but it had to be done by the end of this one day. If at the end of the day there were men not crewed up the chief and his subordinates would organise them into crews. By lunchtime I was in a crew of sorts, and I do not say that sarcastically as you will see later.

Our pilot was F/Sgt Palmer, the navigator Pilot Officer Simons, our bomb aimer was Sgt Pat Jackson, who incidentally had failed the pilots course, but knew a little about flying that might come in handy in an emergency. I was the wireless operator/air gunner. My main job was wireless operator, all the time only going into the turrets, if the gunner is killed or seriously injured. The mid upper gunner was a Welshman called Taffy Harris. The rear gunner was an Irishman called Paddy Shannon who was the oldest man in the crew at 30 years. He used to brag a lot, both at cards and in life and thought he was a real Don Juan. That then was our crew and were stuck with each other, or so we thought. But not for long. After a couple of weeks at Upper Heywood we were moved to the satellite airfield at Barford-St-John to do our flying. This was approximately seven miles from upper Heywood, still our parent airfield and where HF/DF station still controlled us.

More lectures followed. Most especially crew drills for Wellington aircraft, dinghy drill, petrol and oil systems, aircraft layout and under carriage systems, fire, oxygen, parachute drill, intercom and radio telephone, forced landings home and away. These were done, not twice but 12 to 15 times. It had to become automatic in thought and action.

16th June 1944
This was our first flight in the twin engine Wellington with dual control circuits and landings with a staff pilot called Squadron Leader Chown,

who would instruct and show our own pilot how to fly the Wellington. He would do so many take-offs and landings then change places and boy did we notice the difference. He did some terrible landings at first but gradually got better. While this was going on I was getting experience with fixes and bearings and Q codes. All this was important for the navigator to enable him to plot his course. We also did night flights and instrument flying.

20th June 1944

On this day our own pilot took us up for circuits and bumps solo for 1 hour 35 mins. and it seemed ok. And that was the last time we

P/O Rob Simons was the navigator throughout Frankl's tour of operations. 70 years later, Frank was visited by Rob's widow in an emotional reunion (514 Sqn Society).

flew with him. When we landed we handed in our gear and went to lunch, but our pilot was told to report to Station Headquarters and we never saw him again. We never heard what happened. The rest of the crew were called into the Chief Flying Instructors office and told we would be getting a new pilot in a few days. We would continue flying with a staff pilot.

4th July 1944

We were introduced to our new pilot-Flying Officer Hendy. He was good looking and had the quiet, friendly, easy-going personality to go with it. We all took to him and once again a full crew except for a flight engineer. We continued day and night flying and practiced with the cine camera gun exercise with an attacking fighter. A hurricane acted the part.

Now we were on our own except for the first two cross country exercises when a staff pilot accompanied us. Now we were truly on our own.

31

Cross country exercises were now lasting up to 6 hours. I had to listen to Flying Training Command control station for any messages, such as recalls, diversions because of fog or bad weather. If there was nothing they would send a timing signal which we must pick up. If you missed one you were given a good roasting and disciplinary action taken. On a squadron and on operations you had two lots of broadcasts to listen out for, your own group control and bomber command control, that meant two of each, every hour. If you missed one of the broadcasts you could be court-martialled. The only excuse was if the receiver broke down or the operator was seriously injured.

28th July 1944

We were down to do a nickel raid. This was either a leaflet drop or stooging up and down the enemy coast dropping window. Like a spoof raid was on the way also creating mayhem on the enemy radar screens. We were on the latter-a sitting duck for enemy fighters. Of course, there was a full-time raid on as well. It was a long dreary uneventful night.

1st August 1944

I had my first flirtation with the Grim Reaper. We had been on a cross country exercise and everything was fine – until arriving back at base a little early, we found we were still too high about 15,000 feet. I knew we were about to land so I stood up to go to the rear of the aircraft to reel in the long trailing aerial. This is long steel aerial 300 feet long with about 20 lead weights on the end to help stabilise it in the air. This aerial is reeled out once airborne and above 1000 feet. It is used for wireless transmitter work for true bearings and fixes etc. It has to be reeled in well in advance of landing. They are quite valuable and lots of them have been lost due to landing with them still out and being caught in tree branches and hedgerows etc. They swish from side to side and could decapitate anyone on the perimeter of the runway.

To go back. I stood up and could not move. The aircraft was going straight down. The G force was so great I could not sit down. I was just suspended there, gripping parts of the geodetic framework. I couldn't see what was going on as the bulwark door leading to the cockpit was closed. Through that door was the pilot and the bomb aimer or should have been. My position was the first one behind the bulwark door, my equipment immediately aft of the pilot on the separating partition. Just behind me sitting at his table sideways was the navigator and aft of him the mid upper gunner and at the back, the rear gunner. After about three minutes the aircraft seemed to level out of the spin and I carried on to the rear to reel in the aerial. We all looked askance at each other wondering what was going on and what had happened. I radioed the station to say we were coming in to land and closed down. I opened the bulwark door and could not believe my eyes. The front entrance escape hatch was open and no sign of the bomb aimer. The pilot was white and shaking. I plugged in the intercom and asked where Pat was. It was a stupid question. I knew where he should be and where he had gone. I stood there holding on to the door frame with one foot on the spar.

We were still losing height and approaching the runway, almost home now, when it suddenly happened. We touched down on the runway and were careering along when the wheels collapsed or something and she slewed on her belly. A write off. I was flung forward into the nose of the aircraft and how I missed going through the open escape hatch I will never know. I was unconscious and taken to sick quarters. The rest of the information I got from the crew later. When the emergency was over the pilot was put under close arrest. The main danger was fire but that was averted. The bomb aimer who had bailed out turned up four hours later with his parachute and one flying boot under his arm. He'd lost his other boot on the way down. But how he had managed to bale out at all was a miracle and a mystery. He was given a severe reprimand for his actions by not being on the intercom and obeying instructions, which were to help the pilot with combined effort to get the aircraft out of the spin. He said he had seen the pilot waving his hand and thought it had meant for him to get the escape hatch open and get out, which of course was not the case. He said he had seen the earth coming up quickly and thought the rest of us had had it and made a determined effort to get out.

The pilot was reprimanded and given a red endorsement in his log book. A week later, after a court inquiry, we were called into the chief instructor's office. The CO and pilot were there. The chief then asked us point blank, without ceremony, and in front of the pilot, if we as a crew wanted to carry on flying with him. We had previously talked about the possibility of this being put to us, and we all knew it had just

33

been one of those unfortunate things, which occur now and again when flying. So we said yes, and on 8ᵗʰ August we started to fly again. A staff officer accompanied us out on the first two flights, then we were on our own again. After one more flight, our course was completed. There was one more thing to do - the decompression chamber. Not a pleasant experience but it had to be done. We were now free to go into Oxford and enjoy ourselves while we awaited our next posting.

16ᵗʰ August 1944

We were cleared from the station and sent on ten days leave and return to no.1653 Heavy Conversion Unit at RAF Stradishall near Haverhill Suffolk. There we would be flying four engine Stirlings. RAF Stradishill was a permanent airfield with brick buildings etc. It was excellent, but we were only there one night, then moved to a satellite airfield at Chedworth, 6 miles away.

We settled in to the usual lectures on Wireless transmitting procedures and crew drills for Stirlings. The first time we went up to one on the ground what a size it was. The entrance to her innards was on the port side to the rear and up a set of steel ladders. It was a size inside too, plenty of room to move around. When the pilot was in the cockpit he was 22 feet 9 inches from the ground. It was massive, and you wondered how it would ever leave the earth. The pilot, flight engineer (this was where we picked up our flight engineer) and bomb aimer were in the cockpit area. The bomb aimer, when not down in the front for bombing, map reading throwing window out etc. sat in the co-pilots seat and helped him. But on take-off and landings it was the flight engineer, Sgt Ernie Wall who assisted him. Behind the pilot's position sat the navigator at his table, sideways and then I was next to him facing forward with my equipment. My seat was a swivel type with a bullet proof armour plated back and a semi-circular top which rose to about a foot above my head.

15ᵗʰ September 1944

We started flying the aircraft with a staff pilot on board, though our own pilot was flying it and boy were we nervous at first with this giant. We did initial take-off and landings at Tempsford airfield for three and a half hours. It was a lovely aircraft to fly even our Hendy (pilot) was taken with it. But sometimes it could be a bit temperamental on take-off and landings. It had a tendency to swing on take-off, and the undercarriage was a bit problematic at times. It looked ungainly on the ground but like a swan in the air. We continued day and night practice.

28th September 1944

We now took our first cross country flight plus some high-level bombing positions lasting almost six hours. We were having constant practice and feeling confident when on one day we were roaring down the runway and a tyre burst. It shook us rigid as it spun on to the grass turning three times. A lorry transferred our portable equipment to another aircraft and took off without incident.

It was a peculiar life style we were all leading. All things connected with war and destruction. One moment you would be flying or getting ready to fly, things pertaining to death and then soon you would be having a quiet drink in the SGTs mess with no thought of the danger you had just been through or would have to go through again shortly. Life seemed so unreal. Some of us would go for a walk along the country lanes. It was stepping into another world.

Lancasters

The shape of things to come: a line-up of 514 Squadron Lancasters at Waterbeach (Crown Copyright)

14th October 1944

Leave over, I left Darlington bound for No.3 LFS - Lancaster Finishing School at RAF Feltwell in Norfolk. I and four other men were met by RAF transport for the ten-minute drive to camp. I was pleased to see it was a permanent airport with concrete runways. It was still just a grass airfield and for Lancasters too. Still they wouldn't be carrying a full bomb load, just practice bombs, the usual procedures of booking in and finding billets took place. The next day began a week of lectures.

21st October 1944

We commenced our flying on Lancasters. We had a staff pilot F/O Hubbard. We were up on initial dual circuits and landings at nearby at RAF Methwold. This was Feltwell's satellite airfield and they had proper tarmac runways and it was also an operational aerodrome, so we could only practice circuits there when no operations were in progress. The first session was for 2½ hours with F/O Hubbard while our own skipper was doing the actual flying. Then the staff pilot got out at

Feltwell and we were on our own again. Hendy did ok. He was a great pilot and we knit together as a great crew. There was no hassle and we had complete confidence in each other. All we needed 'as every crew did, was Lady Luck riding beside us.'

27th October 1944
We went up in H for How for a fighter affiliation exercise. This was for 40 minutes. No matter how long or short the exercise, it was vital experience, so we never moaned or went on about what a waste of time it was getting our paraphernalia together and getting airborne.

28th October 1944
We did our first night flight on Lancasters. Once again F/O Hubbard accompanied us and this time we went to RAF Foulsham to do circuits and bumps for two hours. The next night we went solo on familiarisation, circuits and landings at Methwold for 2½ hours. The next day was hectic. We were told that the weather being ok they were going to push us and get us finished and through the course by that night, knocking five days off the usual three-week conversion course. Apparently, they were wanting crews for the squadrons. Anyway, at 11am that morning F/O Aitken took us up for a check dual (the pilots benefit) for ten minutes then on our own to the bombing range for a high-level bombing exercise for 50 minutes. Back at the office we found we were down to go on a cross country trip that evening and then we would be finished.

Next day we would be told which operational squadron we had been allocated to. That evening we took off in H for How for our last trip at Feltwell. It was a navigational cross country ending with some high-level bombing then back to base. It took 3½ hours and everything went well.

Now we would be heading for the real thing. But it had been the real thing from day one. From the day we were sworn in. For aircrews, death had been walking at their side every moment, every take-off, every flight the reaper was waiting. In Training Command 15,000 members of aircrew were killed in training for the bombing and destruction of the enemy.

Waterbeach

31st October 1944

We walked down to the flight office and were ushered into the briefing room. All the crews who had finished the course were there and where we were to learn which squadron and airfield we would be going.

We were told we were joining 514 Squadron at Waterbeach, and that it was in No. 3 Group, Bomber Command. We immediately got clearance from different sections on the station and after lunch came to collect us with our kit and drove us to Waterbeach. We said our good byes to the other crews and were on our way. Our kit was very limited to two kit bags per person, one for ordinary clothes and kit the other for flying kit also one or two items of hand luggage for extras.

We liked the new camp immediately. It was permanent RAF station with brick buildings and about five miles from Cambridge and seven miles from Ely. The main road ran along the front of the airfield, consequently people who were aircraft gazing, cars and buses would have to duck their heads if the aircraft were taking off in that direction. Five of us NCOs were billeted in the SGTs mess. It was quite luxurious and comfortable compared to the old Nissan huts we had sometimes had to put up with. Ernie Wall our flight engineer and I had one room and next door were Pat Jackson, the bomb aimer, and Taffy Harris, the mid-upper gunner. The pilot and navigator were in the Officers' Mess nearby.

This was to be our home until we completed 30 operations. We had hope in our hearts and like everyone else we thought it wouldn't happen to us. The Chop! But we knew the odds were stacked against us. That is why aircrew on operational squadrons got six days leave every six weeks. And wonder of wonders-besides being paid your SGT's pay you also got aircrew danger pay of the princely sum of 1 shilling a day. Another perk we received was the customary meal of egg and bacon before every operation and also the same post operational meal on our return-if you returned.

RAF Waterbeach in late 1944, when Frank was stationed there. A large number of Lancasters can be seen at their dispersals. 514 Squadron had up to thirty of the bomber on its strength at this time, making it one of the largest units in Bomber Command (WMHM Dods Collection).

2nd November 1944

On the second day we were interviewed by the CO of the station and also Officer Commanding 514 Squadron. We were given a pep talk, wished the best of luck and that was that.

Now we had to get an operation under our belt then we would be truly accepted into the squadron. Our next priority was to report to our various sections, I to the Signals leader and the signals section.

Flight Lt. Oulton was the Signals chief and he was a gem of a bloke. He was about forty years and affectionately known as Pop. Group Captain C.R. Heard was the Commanding Officer of the camp while Wing Commander Michael Wyatt was the Commanding Officer of 514 Squadron. The squadron was divided into flights-A, B and C. We were assigned to C Flight with Squadron Leader Timms Flight Commander. RAF Waterbeach was a parent station or head station with its own HF/DF wireless transmitting station (High Frequency Direction

514 Squadron wireless operators pose for a group photograph in 1945 (WMHM).

Finding, also known as huff duff) and had two satellite aerodromes, Witchford and Mepal.

Before we could go on our first operation the Skipper had to go on one as second pilot with another crew to give him a little experience and some idea what to expect. This was a night operation somewhere in the Ruhr, so it wouldn't be an easy one. They arrived back unscathed and when we met up with him the next day he shot us a hell of a line.

4th November 1944

It was late in the evening when a battle order was pinned up on the notice board in the Sergeants' Mess and one would also be pinned up in the Officers' Mess. Our pilot's name was on it. So this was it. An early call was booked for 05.15 hrs. This was obligatory. No one was allowed to be late for a briefing. Next morning, dead on the dot at 5.15 am, we were awakened by hammering on the door and 'Wakey, wakey!' bellowed. I was ready with fifteen minutes to spare. I took everything that would identify me or give information away out of my pockets and put it all in my locker. The only identity allowed were the two official discs around our necks. In future this was done at the briefing room. We were given a cloth bag to put everything in and it was reclaimed if and when we returned. I was allowed to take two or three pencils to write in the logs.

At 6am we went to the mess for breakfast. This was usually Corn Flakes or porridge, milk, tea, bread and the coveted bacon and eggs, followed by toast, butter and jam. This was one of the luxuries operational air crew were afforded when going on an operation. It was also the same for the post operational meal except for cereal. If you arrived back in the early hours, sometimes five or six a.m., it wasn't unusual to see someone's plate untouched when leaving the table. Nerves were coming to the fore, butterflies was the usual explanation. But it was more than that. I don't know exactly how you would describe it, but it was a queer feeling one got. Thoughts you tried to put to the back of your mind. It couldn't happen to you, it only happened to other crew. At the same time, you knew DAMNED well it could happen to you, but it never put me off my food. If I was going to get the chop I would do it on a full stomach.

After a final cup of tea and cigarette to steady the nerves it was time to walk down to our respective section headquarters for our own special briefing or pre–briefing. Mine was done by the Stations Signals Leader in the Signals building which was next to the main briefing room. This took about thirty minutes. We would be given all the wireless information, frequencies, call signs for wireless transmitter and radio transmitter colours of the day for the Very cartridge gun, the collective call sign for all 3 Group aircraft and finally the collective call sign for the whole force. All these included both wireless transmitter and radio transmitter call signs. Also, if it was a night raid and there was a Master Bomber, also known as 'master of ceremonies', there would be a special call sign for him and also for his deputy. There was always a Deputy Master Bomber in case the main man was shot down, which did happen now and again.

At 07.30 everyone assembled in the main briefing room. The noise was terrific. Thirty crews, each crew at a separate table. We joined our own pilot and navigator pouring over charts. The total number of crews varied depending whether or not it was to be a maximum effort. We sat there waiting and smoking. We were called to attention as the C.O.s of

41

the station and of 514 Squadron, the respective Flight Commanders and heads of sections walked in. The C.O. immediately put us at ease with "Gentlemen, you may smoke" and the main briefing commenced.

There was a dais at the front of the room and a huge map of Europe on the wall, but it was always covered with a curtain to conceal the route and target. Now the C.O. pulled the curtain back to reveal all. Depending on the target, and /or the length of red tape and number of legs over Europe, there would be howls and groans and various unprintable remarks. Distant and big city targets such as Berlin, Leipzig, Frankfurt, Munich and anything in the Ruhr would not be welcomed. The Ruhr was heavily defended not only with fighter aircraft but a few hundred anti-aircraft guns. It was a hotbed savagely defended right up to the end of the war.

Today, the target was a town called Solingen in the Ruhr where synthetic oil was produced. First we were given the reason for our proposed visit and then each leg of the route was briefed. The exact mileage of each leg, the compass bearing, wind velocity and strict speed to be kept to. We were allocated the height at which our squadron was to fly at and which we had to stick to unless there were unforeseen circumstances cropping up and necessitated a change. These had to be valid, consequential reasons for doing so. All the flak area positions and fighter airfields en-route were marked. Each leg of the route being as far as possible from these positions. We were told our bomb load was to be; one 4000 lb Cookie or blockbuster plus, for this medium distant target, ten 1000lb high explosive bombs. This was our usual load. Sometimes it varied. Most likely a 4000lb cookie plus ten or twelve cans of incendiary bombs. The further away the target the less bomb load and more high-octane petrol to get us back again. A Lancaster could carry 2150 gallons if required.

Next we would be given on all the information on the total number of aircraft and types that would be operating on the raids, from which groups they would come, which wave we would be in, at what height we would fly and also our time on target (T.O.T). Then, at our own Squadron and Flight level, we would be told which other aircraft we would be flying with and the letters on the side of the aircraft of these.

42

As our navigator had been specially trained on radar we were a G.H. leader and therefore three other aircraft would be looking out for us, so they could formate on us. We would be in charge of them. On the run in to the target they had to copy what we did; when our bomb doors opened they had to open theirs and when they observed us dropping our bombs they had to drop theirs. We had to fly straight and level until they had all bombed. Once on the bombing run it was my job to get into the astronomers, watch these three Lancasters formating on us and tell the pilot once they had dropped their loads. I also had to watch out for aircraft above us. There were never supposed to be directly overhead but somehow there always were. There was always supposed to be three minutes between the first and second waves, but over such a distance and time that gap became non-existent. Heights for each wave would typically start at 23000 feet for the first couple of squadrons and then reduce by 500ft each time down to a minimum of 19000ft. Then the second wave commenced starting at the higher altitude. Frequently one or two squadrons at the end of the first wave, at the minimum altitude of around 19000 feet, would be overtaken by the first couple of squadrons of the second wave who were at the higher altitude of around 23000 feet. It was nothing new or strange to be bombed from above by our own aircraft. Tragically, many bombers were lost in this way.

*In fact, this risk had been present throughout the night bombing campaign but until the advent of mass daylight raids, RAF crews had been spared the sought of this menace.

We would be informed of other raids taking place that day and what fighter escort we could expect either for the whole way or just part of the way.

All this would be told to us by the C.O. of 514 Squadron and the Intelligence Officer. Next would come the Navigation Leader, then the Bomb Aimer Leader, next the Signals Officer, the Gunnery Leader and finally it would be the turn of the Met man giving us all the weather expected going over and on our return plus the U.F.E???

. At the end of the briefing the Station Commander would say a few words and wish everyone the best of luck. At that point you would be

A wireless operator at his position in a Lancaster. The benefit was its proximity to the heater outlet (Crown Copyright).

given final instructions on the runway in use, the time you had to enter your aircraft, time for starting your engines and checking everything, time to start taxiing to the runway in use. Time to for the first aircraft out to take-off was finally done by the Flying Control Tower and also the control van at the end of the runway by giving the green light for take-off. But back to the main briefing. As soon as it was over the room was filled with babble. It was like a saloon with the blue haze of cigarette smoke and everyone was talking at once. By that time, it was about 8.45 am, time to go to the nearby locker room to get into our flying kit, draw our parachute and Mae West whilst one of the crew drew the flying rations. Then each crew member had to draw and sign for his emergency escape kit at the intelligence office. This consisted of emergency rations such as chocolate, Horlicks tablets, sea water purifying tablets, hard biscuits, two or three small condensed maps of Europe for escape purposes, and money in German, French, Belgium and Dutch currency. These escape packages were in a hard plastic see-through box to be handed in on return to base. We then had to test our oxygen masks on the portable testers in the crew room.

In the wireless operator's position in a Lancaster where I sat, the opening for the hot air sent from the engines was directly opposite me and, while other members of the crew like the mid upper and rear gunners were usually freezing, I was sometimes sweating. Those in the cockpit were usually just about warm enough. I usually flew in my ordinary battle dress uniform, a black wool sweater, thick black wool socks and my flying boots. I took two pairs of gloves, one pair chamois leather and one pair pure silk, in case I needed them. They had to be thin in order to write my Wireless transmitter log in pencil but I in fact I rarely had to wear any.

When everyone had got themselves sorted out and into crews again, we assembled outside the crew rooms waiting for the transport that would take us out to our aircraft at dispersal. Sometimes a dispersal would be at the other side of the airfield, maybe a mile or a mile and half away. Drivers were always WAAFs. they were a good-humoured lot, joking, but aware of what we may be feeling. Three crews at a time were taken in the lorries and dropped off near their aircraft. We were dropped off at C for Charlie and had about twenty minutes to spare before the official time of getting in and starting up.

The two pieces of equipment above are the R1155 receiver (left) and the T1154 transmitter (right). Thousands of these radios were made and many still exist and, indeed, work well.

Immediately the pilot went round the plane checking, making sure as far as was possible at this stage that everything was OK. The rest of the crew entered and went to their positions depositing their parachutes and equipment. Personally, I had to squeeze past the bottom of the mid-upper gun turret over the main spar which served as my seats back rest, stow my parachute in the container next to my seat and checked my satchel. This contained pencils, W/T log, Q code book, Bomber Command code book and some sheaves of rice paper with other secret information on. These had to be chewed up and swallowed if we were forced down in enemy territory. I made sure everything was working, switching on the R1155 receiver and listening to the signals coming through my helmet head set. I switched on the T1154 to make sure the valves were heating up and quickly pressed the Morse key. I ensured the intercom was working and also checked the trailing aerial and earth connections including the HF fixed aerial leads from outside to the aerial board inside. That was all for now. When all checks were completed we gathered outside chatting to the ground crew and have our last smoke before the off.

As time drew near stomachs started to churn and adrenalin flowed. But there was an inner excitement too. I cant explain but ask any operational air crew and they would confirm the peculiar feeling one got. All we had trained for (23 months in my case) was now going into the boiling pot. Anyone who said he wasn't scared was either a liar or there was something lacking in his makeup. I am trying to explain the feelings one has. It is a mixture of a love for flying, excitement, fear, proud to be fighting for your country, camaraderie with men as crews. You lived for this day, that's all because you knew the chances of your completing a tour was slim. We knew what we were letting ourselves in for. There was no turning back. No L.M.F. for us. Time passed quickly on. Dead on 09.30hrs we dumped our cigarettes and climbed into the aircraft. The entry door was at the rear of the aircraft just before the tail plane and rudders on the starboard side. There was a small steel ladder about six rungs and this was drawn in and stowed by the last man in, usually one of the gunners. I put on my helmet with oxygen mask and microphone attached and waited for the pilot and the ground crew to start up the engines. My wireless equipment and electrical circuits were powered by large accumulator batteries charged constantly by engine driven generator (E.D.G.) in the starboard inner engine. Outside, the ground staff would attach a trolley battery, set to start up the engines so as not to drain the power from the aircrafts batteries. The pilot would signal to them which engine he was starting up then would press the button for that engine. The propellers would slowly start to turn and then, with a staccato burst of noise, would fire and burst into thunderous life. It was a sound vibrant with the emotion of power and when the four of them were running it was like sweet music to the ears. But loud, and I mean loud!

Once the motors were running I switched my equipment on, making sure once again everything was o.k. I wouldn't commence my w/t watch until we were airborne. I made sure the flare chute and the flares were secure also the Very pistol and cartridges with the correct colours of the day. Then I sat there waiting and watching and listening to the usual paraphernalia that went on at this time. Each engine would be revved up to maximum to check it was running o.k. no mag drops or oil pressure problems, no overheating etc. After each engine was run on its own all four throttles would be opened up to clear each engine and what a din! If everything was to the skipper's satisfaction, he gave the thumbs up to the ground crew, who would have previously disconnected the trolley accumulator before engines were run up. They would pull the chocks away ready for us to taxi out. The skipper would then check with each crew member to affirm that everyone and everything was checked and ok and especially that every position's oxygen supply was working, and the intercom was in order.

At precisely 10.00 hrs we started to move out of our dispersal and the ground crew gave us the thumbs up and wished us good luck. Nearly all the aircraft round the field were moving around the perimeter track to the beginning of the runway in use. On the side of the runway was the controller's black and white chequered van. This was where the take-off control was done, by the green light from the Aldis lamp rather than by radio transmitter from the control tower. The take-off time of each Lancaster was recorded in a log in the control van with the letter of the aircraft and time then passed by landline telephone to the control tower where it was logged again.

One Lancaster was lined up on the end of the runway waiting for the green light to be given for clear to take-off. There were two others in front of us. Butterflies were churning now. This was it. Take-off with full bomb load and petrol load was one of the most fateful moments. Anything could happen. So many causes. Any unknown reason. That was why your heart was in your mouth and you sweated!

At last our turn came. The Lancaster on the runway started to move forward ever so slowly and began to pick up speed. It was travelling fast now and slowly its tail wheel came up then suddenly it was airborne. We turned on the runway and the brakes squealed as we came to a halt all lined up, dead centre, ready for take-off. The skipper called us all up in turn on the intercom asking if we were ready and then, on receiving the green light, said "Right, here we go." Brakes full on, he pushed the four throttle levers slowly up, nearly to the fully open position and the engines roared! He released the brakes and slowly we began to move down the runway. There were always a few officers, air men and women by the side of the control van to watch the take-offs and they would give us the thumbs up as we set off. In fact, you could see little groups of personnel scattered all over watching the take-off. The main road from Cambridge to Ely that ran along the whole length of the airfield was full of cars pulled up on hard standing, people and sometimes a bus, all watching.

I was sitting at my position looking out of the little rectangular window at my left-hand side watching the huge Merlin engines and the two propellers, which were just a blur. I was sweating with tension. Slowly we gathered speed and then we were roaring down the runway. The throttles were opened fully now, and the roar of the engines increased. You could feel the extra surge in power. Now we were at the point of no return. We were committed to the take-off. Faster she went, the tail went up and we kept going. The end of the runway looming up with the ditch at the end of it and the road with the spectators watching. Then with relief, suddenly we were airborne. What a lovely feeling. I started my wireless transmitter watch then noting the time we were airborne in the log, the E.D.G. readings, voltage and current of the accumulators. Looking at my watch I checked how long I had before tuning in for the 3 Group H.Q broadcast, which used wireless transmitter call sign 35/3 on 3190k c/s. These were sent on the hour and half-hour for three minutes. If they had no information for us they just sent call signs and identifying figures for late tuners. The number was included so logs could be checked that no broadcast was missed. This could be a chargeable offence. At quarter to and quarter past the hour, broadcasts from H.Q. Bomber Command had to be picked up by w/t. There were nearly always winds that were transmitted and every navigator in the main force had to use them. This was also usually a three-minute transmission time. Now that we had gained height I could reel out the 300-foot trailing aerial weighted at the end with fifteen lead balls to prevent swinging beneath the aircraft. The steel wire aerial was on a winch near my left hand.

We started to climb to our orbit height about 5,000 feet and continued orbiting waiting for our followers. Sometimes we had two followers, other times three. We knew their aircraft code letters and they would know ours; also, they knew us as G.H. aircraft by the two broad yellow stripes painted on our tail fins for identification purposes. These yellow stripes could be seen from quite a distance away, so aircraft could see a G.H. leader aircraft initially and converge to see if it was their leader.

Within five minutes we had our three followers tagging along, all just aft of us, one on the port side, one on the starboard side, and one in the middle rear forming a kind of diamond. The one in the middle would fly a little lower or higher to avoid the wash of our propellers. Everywhere I looked now, I could see little formations all over the sky and, here and there, a few loose Lancasters frantically dashing hither and thither looking for their leaders. Then at a certain time, 10.30 hrs on this occasion, it was time to set course for Germany, and Solingen. It was an amazing sight. All those Lancasters setting off for the Ruhr. I believe the main force on this raid totalled about 700. This would include Lancasters and Halifaxes from 4, 5 and 6 Groups which would converge with us over the North Sea.

Immediately we set off on the actual first leg. We gained height up to 20,000 feet for our Squadron. As we had been circling over Cambridgeshire at about 5,000 feet it would take another half to three-quarters of an hour to get up to our allocated height. Once we reached 10,000 feet it was time to put our oxygen masks and microphones to be permanently fastened up on to the helmet. From now on we would be getting two or three puffs of pure oxygen every minute until we reduced height again, usually as we approached the enemy coast homeward bound.

Now my job was routine. Receiving the wireless transmission broadcasts from 3 Group and also Bomber Command. This would be every fifteen minutes for each. The winds from Bomber Command were passed immediately to the navigator. Everything was going smoothly but everyone was alert, expecting the unexpected. Hours of routine en-route to the target. The pilot would, of course, be flying the aircraft; the navigator still plotting his route and keeping track of just where we were or where we were supposed to be. The bomb aimer would be either helping the pilot or map reading to help the navigator with his pin points. The flight engineer would still be checking the engine gauges and

49

temperatures also fuel amounts left. Gunners would be searching the sky for enemy aircraft or anything unusual. No one could relax completely until we were back on Terra Firma.

Back to the route out. On the route to the target there would generally be three or four legs, basically to try and fool the enemy fighters and the radar controllers as to which was the actual target destination. After bombing it would be precisely the same legs home. If there was trouble in any form the quickest route in a straight line could be taken making sure hot spots were by passed if possible. The noise of the four Merlin engines throbbing away was terrific and you did get used to it. The helmet cut down the din a little.

Sometimes you would see the target well under attack long before you were anywhere near it if the weather was clear but if it was dense cloud bombing would be by sky markers and you would never see the ground or target. You knew it was there. Flak would be coming up thick and fast just before the bombing run. I would get into the astrodome and observe our followers and any aircraft who might just be flying above us or somewhere near.

We were now on our bombing run and very vulnerable as we had to fly straight and level as well as getting on the correct heading. I was listening on the crew intercom hearing the dialogue between the pilot navigator and bomb aimer and also watching our followers. I then heard "Bomb doors open" and started to sweat knowing that any hit from flak now either direct, or just hot shrapnel on the blockbuster, would send us to kingdom come. The navigator could now be heard directing the pilot and the bomb aimer as we were G.H. Then bombs away. I was observing our followers and saw them release their bomb loads at precisely the same time as us. After a few more seconds to allow for photos to be taken by the automatic camera, we wheeled out of the target area like bats out of hell with our formation still following behind.

The flak was still coming up fast and furious and it was getting quite accurate. At times too close for comfort. A salvo would suddenly burst just beneath you or under the wing and you would hear the crump, crump, crump and the shrapnel clumping against the fuselage. Besides the firing of the ack-ack now was the time to look out for enemy fighters. Just after leaving the target on the first leg home was the most perilous, although anytime on any leg they could be expected. I was back in my seat and listening out for one of Group's broadcasts. I'd only been off the wireless for about seven or eight minutes and I hadn't missed any broadcasts. There was nothing for us just the check number and a timing signal. The steady thrump, thrump of the engines was like a drug making me feel quite sleepy. After flying for about an hour after leaving the target we began to feel a little easier, though nobody was complacent.

I had already eaten the flying ration sandwiches and chocolate on the way out, so I poured myself the last of the thermos coffee –nice, hot and sweet. It was a lovely feeling once you crossed the French or Dutch coast going home. Now you would be down to about 10,000 feet gradually losing height so as to cross the English coast at about 6,000 feet. We would probably cross in at Aldeburgh in Suffolk then we would lose height quickly in daytime and scoot back for home at about 2,000 feet. It would only take fifteen to twenty minutes back to base at Waterbeach and I had the aerial to wind in. Looking out of my side window I knew we were near home just five minutes and I knew the pilot was in touch with base flying control, so I closed down the radio transmitter and entered it in my log. I then switched myself on to the intercom position with the rest of the crew and heard the skipper calling Waterbeach Flying Control. He was asking permission to join the circuit. Flying Control acknowledged giving him permission to join the circuit, giving him barometric pressure and also the height to fly in the circuit and what number our turn was to land.

Any aircraft in trouble would be given priority to land. It wasn't long before it was our turn Flying Control called us up and informed us of the number of runway in use according to wind direction and told us to lose height to 1000 feet. Then the skipper told them when he had turned into funnels, that is, turned into the heading to land on the runway gradually losing height all the time. Flight Control would tell him to pancake, land, which Hendy did with expertise. We had great faith in him as a pilot and trust in each other. After landing we taxied round to dispersal and after giving the engines one more run to clear them they were closed down. What a QUIETNESS. The ground staff were there waiting. They gave us the thumbs up sign and put the chocks under the wheels.

The sudden silence was deafening in its intensity. It was strange not to be hearing the roar of those Merlins. I entered in my log the time of landing and signed that all the equipment was ok and serviceable. I put all my bits of paper, log and code books into the satchel, picked up my parachute and started to clamber towards the rear door looking to make sure there were no flares in the chute as I passed. I climbed down the ladder, whipped my helmet off and kissed Mother Earth. Our first operation was over. My legs felt strange after being airborne for four or five hours (4 hrs 50 mins. exactly) and your head seemed tight and ringing. The first thing we did was to pull our cigs out and have one and wasn't it lovely? The transport for us came quickly and we all climbed aboard to go to the de-briefing room for interrogation.

On arrival we were offered a large mug of hot sweet steaming tea and also a double tot of rum. We were shown to a table and all seated. There were free cigarettes on the table that were just to smoke at the table. An intelligence officer sat down with us and asked all manner of questions. We all gave him information of what we had seen. It would all be checked and double checked. This took about 30 minutes. Our escape kits were handed in and then to the locker room to take-off our flying gear. We then received our own personal belongings in a fabric bag, went on to Parachute Section and handed in our chutes. The parachute harness and Mae West stayed with our flying kit. Then it was off to the Sergeants' Mess for our meal of egg and bacon a smoke and a chat and then off to bed for a couple of hours.

We were glad and relieved to have the first op over now we felt like we belonged with the squadron we were operational at last. I would like to try and explain how we felt, in the realities and meanings that came to me. It became like a drug. Even though you felt scared you looked forward to the next one. There was the excitement and exhilaration of flying, the build-up of tensions, the danger, even just the take-offs with a full bomb load, the atmosphere, the whole thing. I suppose I can never explain the feelings at such a time.

6th November 1944

Next day was a day off. It was an official 'Stand Down' till midnight so I went to look round at the City of Cambridge for the first time. It was smaller than I thought. I caught the last bus home at 10.30 pm.

7th November 1944

We did some practice photo bombing and some Fighter affiliation practice. In the evening a Battle Order was pinned up and later taken down. The next two days were quiet.

10th November 1944.

A Battle Order was put up and we were on it. Flying breakfast was scheduled for 0400 hours. Pre–briefing at 1450 hours, main briefing 0530 hours, transport 0700 hours, into aircraft at 0730 hours, taxi out at 0800 hours and first aircraft off about 0805 hours. Everything meticulously timed.

Our aircraft was 'C' Charlie and we were in 'C' flight. The target this time was Castrop Rauxel, an oil plant. There would be 400 Lancasters and 100 Halifaxes. Once again we were a G.H. leader with three Lancasters formating on us. They would be a fighter escort with us, but they would fly way above us at 30,000 feet while we kept at our usual 21,000 feet. The fighters were Spitfires and Mustangs and the usual German fighters they met in daylight were FW 190s and ME 109s.

Flak was always present especially if we passed close to heavily defended town or city. Sometimes it was quite thick and accurately predicted. We noticed Lancasters in trouble. One was running on three engines, one being feathered and still on fire. Another had its port wing on fire and was going down, whilst a bit further along on our starboard side a formation of Lancasters being victimised by the radar predicted flak and getting hell knocked out of them over the target. I got the screaming Hab Dabs! We were on our bombing run. There were too many aircraft, some only 50 feet above us, with their bomb doors open, also running in to the target. I nearly had kittens. I yelled at Hendy over the intercom alerting him to the danger and to edge over to port. We gradually moved over and 'flip a lid', if the other aircraft didn't do likewise. I told the skipper and he moved quickly to starboard. Just seeing those blockbusters and their bombs hanging there above us waiting to be released any moment wasn't doing me any good at all. Thankfully we got clear of them just as they fell away and at the same time we released our load. I noticed our followers, who were still with us dropped their contribution too. I informed the skipper and after allowing for the automatic camera he swung out from the target and on to the course for the first leg home. I had a last look round in the astrodome and what a sight to see all those Lancasters and Halifaxes some still in formation like us, others on their own and looking backwards the black bursts of anti- aircraft fire.

I resumed watch on my set and was just in time to get a Bomber Command broadcast. There were sent out at fifteen words a minute so even the poorest operator could take it down. Once over the Suffolk coast, Hendy reduced height and flew in at low level at 200 feet, our three followers formating on us. We weren't supposed to fly this low but some of us did now and again. It gave us a lift when people in the villages and fields stood waving to us. We arrived back at Waterbeach at 12.55 hours, so we had been airborne 4 hours 55 minutes. As soon as we had taxied round to our dispersal point the transport was waiting for us. We had a quick look for damage and shrapnel holes. We found a few in the tail plane, then we were taken for interrogation. Within an hour we were having our return flying meal. Then we relaxed and began to wind down during the afternoon. It took a little time to get back to normal feelings of being back on the ground again and to get the ringing out or your head and ear.

The following days were quiet. We flew test and practice flights and the squadron took delivery of some new Lancasters that had to be checked and tested. These quiet times gave the ground crew time to check and repair the aircraft before the next operation.

16th November 1944
It was nine days before the next battle order was pinned up, at which it was camp shut down. All personnel were now confined to camp. No one was allowed in or out and no private phone calls were permitted till after the raid. Our flying breakfast was scheduled for 08.45 hours, pre-briefing 09.15 hours, main briefing 10.30 hours, transport 12 noon, into

aircraft 12.30 hours, start to taxi out 13.00 hours, first one to take-off as soon as possible. The first aircraft, the one nearest the runway in use, would be airborne at 13.05 hours. After breakfast we went into what was becoming a familiar routine. At the main briefing the map of Europe was unveiled showing the red strings marking the outward legs and the return legs. It was another trip to the Ruhr, a town called Heinsburg producing synthetic oil from two or three plants. Our aircraft, again, was 'C' for Charlie. The pilot, navigator and bomb aimer were already at the table with the navigator drawing in his route on the Mercator chart – tracking legs to the target and back. All the relevant information he had at the moment would be shortly be jotted down. The navigator had a lot of work to do besides listening to the briefing. He would be working out everything connected with the route right up to the time for putting on his flying suit.

We did not know at the time that this was to be the raid on which we would lose our friends. We were third in line for take-off with a five-ton bomb load. Our engines were throbbing just waiting. Then Hendy said 'Here we go. 'The engines roared, and we were belting down the runway. Then we were airborne. After orbiting for a few minutes, we rendezvoused with our three followers. Ten minutes later, we were off to set course and gain height. It took another thirty minutes to reach 20,000 feet. I got up to look out the astrodome. There were 400 Lancasters on this operation and everywhere I looked I could see the little formations. It was time to sit down and tune in the receiver to get the group broadcasts. Now and again I looked out of my side window. We were over Germany with no cloud. The fields, villages and towns looked like toys.

As soon as we neared the Ruhr we began to get anti-aircraft fire that could be from 100 to 300 guns having a go at you and it would be radar predicted flak, the worst kind. Altogether in the Ruhr area there were 1,000 ack-ack guns. The barrages around the big cities such as Essen and Cologne were terrific.

Five minutes to the run in on target I took my place in the astrodome as observer watching our followers. I heard the navigator say, 'We are on the bombing run'. Next thing we heard was 'Bombs away.' The followers on the port and rear dropped theirs with us but the starboard ones hadn't released. I informed the skipper and we continued to fly straight and level a little longer. I kept my eyes on them. Then I saw three black shapes drop away. In the next moment there was a hell of an explosion and the blast threw us all over the place. When we sorted ourselves out and looked back there was only a huge black cloud hanging in the sky where our mates had been. The pilot was Australian, and the crew were our special friends. Blown up and just vanished. It was unbelievable. Where our other two followers were, we had no idea. We just kept plugging on for home. We did not know if we had sustained any damage, but the aircraft seemed to be flying alright. We were a shaken crew when we landed at base and told the ground crew what had happened. They were upset because they had known that crew very well. Their dispersal was next to ours.

The dispersals were nearly always in a group of three. Each dispersal was a concrete circle approximately 30 yards apart, connected to the same strip of tarmac leading out on to the airport perimeter and so to the runways. One of our ground crew went over to their ground crew and told them they wouldn't be coming back and explained what had happened.

At the de-briefing, each of us had to describe what we had seen and nothing more. There would be an inquiry and every aspect would be explored and they would announce their opinions and findings into what had happened. The result of the inquiry was that there was a fault in the electrical circuit in the bomb aimers panel and therefore he had to jettison the bomb load. But a mistake had been made. Instead of dropping the blockbuster on its own, first or last, and then the 500lb bombs separately, he had jettisoned the lot together and one of the 500lb bombs cannoned against the blockbuster as it was leaving the bay and caused the explosion. The crew wouldn't have known a thing about it.

2nd December 1944

It was decided just in case the pilot was killed or seriously injured some of the crew should have some knowledge on how to handle the controls and have some chance of keeping the aircraft airborne and hope ground staff could talk it down. The flight engineer, bomb aimer and myself were chosen from our crew and given some instruction. If this became impossible one man would stay at the controls while the rest of the crew baled out over the base area. The remaining man would guide the plane out to sea, which was only fifteen minutes away, bale out and let the aircraft crash into the sea. We had three lessons. It was great flying a Lancaster, but we were never solely in control. The pilot was always there.

4th December 1944

We went to Oberhausen bombing railway yards.

5th December 1944

Another Ruhr trip to Hamm where the target was extensive marshalling yards which required our attention. This was a daylight operation. All Ruhr targets were heavily defended. Hamm seemed to be extraordinarily so. It was a den of iniquitous flak.

6th December 1944

Things really did happen, especially for me, on this trip. We were on our way to Merseburg near Leipzig. It was a night raid on oil refineries. We were airborne at 16.52 hours and had only been flying about an hour when the intercom broke down. I managed to get the emergency intercom into service, so the skipper decided to press on. No sooner was that panic over when ten minutes later the wireless transmitter broke down. The 'magic eye' was still alight (green) The tuning valve by which you tune the T1154 transmitter by back-tuning to the receiver signal obtaining deflection in the 'magic eye'. This ensures you are dead on to the frequency and getting maximum power output at the same time. In a case like this I had to inform the skipper that the transmitter was useless. I had approximately half an hour to repair it. If that was not possible the pilot must not press on but had to return to base. With the 'magic eye' lit up it showing power was there, so it had to be a faulty valve somewhere. I informed the skipper who told me to try and fix it because he did not want to turn back now. We were crossing the Dutch coast going in. There wasn't much room to work in. We only had a small table on which to write our W/T log and also a Morse code key on the edge of it. Such were the difficulties that faced you when something went wrong. I switched the power off and unscrewed the fixing screws on the receiver. The only light I had was a low wattage lamp fixed to a folding and extending arm. I pulled the receiver chassis out of its container and tried to fathom out what had gone wrong. I thought at first it might be one of the I.F. valves and tried each in turn by shorting one out but it wasn't either. I had to take a chance. It must be the output valve and there were no spares and it couldn't be substituted by any of the obvious valves - not even the D/F portion of the receiver. I looked at the pins on the 'magic eye' valve and they appeared to be identical. The only snag there was no connector caps on it and there was on the output valve. I decided to take a chance. As I pulled the output valve out of its socket, it broke at its base. It was sink or swim now. I got it all out of its socket then pulled the 'magic eye' out of its holder then out of its base. I inserted this into the output valves position and just laid the lead from the previous valve on to the top of the lead. Before pushing the receiver back into its container, I tried it out. I pushed the power plugs back into their sockets and switched on, waited for them to warm up for a few seconds and crossed my fingers. Hey Presto, it was working. I was just in time to receive a group broadcast. It was working again but I was on tenterhooks the whole of the flight as we had 6½ hours to go before we were safe home again. Back at base it was reported, and the Signals Leader was most impressed.

Life on the squadron was pleasant enough but so unpredictable. One moment you were living an ordinary kind of service life and then suddenly with the appearance of a Battle Order going up on the mess notice board the adrenalin started to flow, and nerves were fluttering. Within a few hours everyday things would be insignificant and life would take on a totally different aspect. Our lives would be filled with carnage both delivering and receiving and sometimes it would be like going through hell itself. From the moment the order was posted apprehension, excitement and fear walked side by side with you. It was only when you returned the tension eased and you could begin to relax- till the next time.

514 Squadron Lancasters formate on their GH Leader (note stripes on tail fins) on the daylight raid to Siegen on 16th December 1944 (Harry Dison, Lancasters at Waterbeach, Bomber Command Books).

16th December 1944

There was an odd incident connected to our next incursion to the Fatherland. We were briefed for a daylight trip to Siegen. The target was railway yards. The weather was atrocious. It was patchy fog and mist and no aircraft should ever have taken off. It seemed this target should be dealt with immediately, but they were sending only G.H. trained crews. It looked odds on that we wouldn't be able to land at our base on our return. We took off at 11.21 hours had an uneventful journey there and back. We bombed ok but, apparently some aircraft had not dropped their bombs and had to unload them into the North Sea on the way back. This is where the odd bit came in. On the same day, band leader Glen Miller set off to Paris in a light aircraft and disappeared. They should never have set off. Rumour had it that it was hit accidentally by one of the bombs jettisoned by the Lancasters over the sea. We couldn't understand why some Lancasters hadn't dropped their bombs on the target.

21st December 1944

We were briefed for a raid on Trier. Information was that the town was packed with German troops and we were to obliterate it. There were 400

Lancasters and Halifaxes with full bomb loads on this raid and it was really plastered.

23rd December 1944
Another battle order was pinned up. At the main briefing on the 23rd we naturally glanced at the map to see where those red legs were taking us and were surprised to see once again it was Trier to finish it off and also supporting our own troops who were converging on the town but still ten miles away. The Germans had also brought more panzer divisions into the town and the area lying in wait for them. The bomber force was about the same size again but no Halifaxes from 4 or 6 group this time. There couldn't have been a building left after this second raid. The weather was terrible over Christmas - a lot of fog and impossible to fly so we were able to enjoy Christmas dinner and have a pleasant day.

28th December 1944
This was a daylight raid to Cologne with a lot of flak and aircraft were wheeling all over the sky trying to find a safe way through - it had to be endured. We arrived back unscathed. We had done fifteen ops including the skippers flight for experience. We were hailed as one of the experienced crews.

31st December 1944
On New Year's Eve we took part in a daylight raid on Vohwinkle. The target was marshalling yards. So ended 1944[1].

1st January 1944
Vohwinkle again. Back to the marshalling yards. A night flight this time, which is a

New Years' Eve 1944 and a good time was had by all at this party at Waterbeach. All, that is, except for the Hendy crew who were sent to bed early to improve their bombing accuracy!

---

[1] *Rob Simons' wife related how there was a station party to celebrate the New Year. However, the Hendy crew had not bombed with any great accuracy so had been ordered to have an early*

totally different experience. You fly in complete darkness knowing there are 400 to 700 aircraft in the stream all on the same heading, going to the same target. You turned on to the runway. It was dark. There were blue lights on both sides of the perimeter track for taxiing and various red, yellow, green lights along the sides of the runway in use, denoting how much runway was left to get airborne. All high buildings such as towers and hangers etc. had red lights to warn low flying aircraft.

Once the last aircraft is airborne all lights are switched off except the PUNDIT. This was a continuously flashing identification beacon - two letter – red that let pilots know which airfield it was. This was a great help to aircraft returning from raids. The Waterbeach beacon was WJ. Lights were switched on as soon as the first aircraft crossed the Suffolk coastline.

Tonight, on our way to Vohwinkle, I was in a world of my own listening for broadcasts. I would be concentrating on using the 'Fish Pond' radar, watching for fast moving blips which denoted fighter aircraft in the stream. The gunners would have to make sure they weren't Mosquitos mixed in with the bomber stream and mistaken for intruders etc. When I peeped out of the window from the side of the curtain I wondered how the German fighters couldn't see us. There they were, two huge Merlin engines roaring away. The exhaust steel was glowing red/white hot as were all the hundreds of others. They were partially covered over on top, but that glow was a real giveaway. But apparently not. On a clear night you could see the flashes of guns and seconds later the explosion, a burst of flame, crump, crump, crump and a splattering of shrapnel against the aircraft. I always had to look out the astrodome when approaching the target and on the bomb run. Most times it was hell on earth both down there and up here too.

When I allowed myself to think like that, I felt sorry for those on the ground especially for the children. However, the majority of the adult population supported the Nazi regime and they were as arrogant and

---

night in order to improve their accuracy. This disappointed Mrs. Simons who had travelled to Waterbeach specially for the occasion.

The wireless operator's equipment in a Lancaster. Top is the T1154 transmitter. The set with the large semi-circular dial is the R1155 receiver. On the left, the smaller set with the circular screen is the 'Fishpond' which used the H2S signal to detect other aircraft, especially those belonging to the Luftwaffe.

egotistical as Hitler and his henchmen. They knew as well as anyone the horrors committed in their name including indescribable crimes and atrocities perpetrated in concentration camps. They didn't care about women and children killed in air raids over Poland, France, Belgium, Holland, Rotterdam razed to the ground along with London, Coventry, Liverpool and Bristol. They didn't worry about how they suffered. The final argument was, 'What it would be like if the Germans won?' We would be a country of slaves and face extermination.

Approaching Vohwinkle the flak was intense and search lights were numerous and very active. The ordinary search lights had a yellowish beam but there were two in this bunch that had a bluish light. These were radar controlled. Once they latched on to an aircraft it was nearly impossible to shake it off. Immediately it had you in its beam all the other searchlights swung on to you and the flak concentrated on that poor unfortunate aircraft in the apex of their lights. Nine times out of ten the aircraft was doomed. It either exploded in the air or went spinning down in flames. It was possible to escape the relentless beam

514 SQUADRON, R.A.F., WATERBEACH, 1945

by putting the nose down, go like the clappers, pull up, swing all over the place and go like hell again and with luck get out of it.

The raid was uneventful over the target but returning over southern Holland we were fired on by American anti-aircraft guns. We took a risk of German fighters being around and fired off the colours of the day and they didn't stop. Our language was blue. We cursed them and called them all the silly buggers under the sun. At the de-briefing we played merry hell. Next day we flew as passengers to Woodbridge to fly back one of our Lancasters that had made an emergency landing after being badly shot up. Woodbridge was one of three aerodromes especially adapted for this purpose. It was equipped with FIDO. The runway was mile long and 3 times the normal width. Manston in Kent and Carnaby in Yorkshire were the other two.

3rd January 1945

Today we went on a daylight trip to Dortmund in the Ruhr. The target was to obliterate the town. There was plenty of flak and one scarecrow[2] thrown up at us. The weather was foul. It was dark and rain pelting

---

[2] A scarecrow was something the Germans fired up by anti-aircraft gun. It exploded just like an ordinary shell leaving behind a pall of smoke and flame and things falling out like parts of an aircraft. It was just as dangerous as a shell It was supposed to demoralise the crews into thinking one of our aircraft had gone down. It actually appeared that way. You couldn't tell the difference.

down, and we were afraid we would collide with another returning aircraft, but we landed safely.

4th January 1945
We were briefed for a raid on Ludwigshafen, but it was cancelled.

5th January 1945
We were briefed for Ludwigshafen again. The target was marshalling yards. It was a long way into southern Germany and reputed to be heavily defended. It was two towns separated by a river like Newcastle and Gateshead, but much larger. On the right side of the river was Mannheim. With our two followers we crossed the Belgium coast and the cloud cleared but with the coldness in the air and at this height the engines were leaving four contrails a dead giveaway to those on the ground. We were supposed to have fighter escort, but we didn't see any. This was the worst flak we had ever seen. I was glad when we had bombed, and I could get out of the astrodome and back in my seat, even though the thought of it as a safer place was just an illusion. This was a six-hour trip.

6th January 1945
We were on again. This time it was to Neuss, in the Ruhr. We were joined at the Dutch coast by a force of Halifaxes from Yorkshire. Once again, the target was marshalling yards. It was an uneventful trip. During the following days we were called upon to do snow clearing.

11th January 1945
It was still overcast but at last it had stopped snowing and visibility had improved but the cloud was low. Amazingly, there was a raid on. It must have been urgent to fly in these conditions. The target was marshalling yards at Krefeld. When we reached 20,000 feet it was good to see blue sky. Because of the cloud when we reached the target we couldn't see it and had to drop sky markers and bomb on them. We never saw the ground until we reached the Suffolk coast coming home.

Wing Commander Michael Wyatt, DFC (front row, centre) was CO of 514 Squadron for most of Frank's time with the unit. He was popular with his crews. After leaving the squadron in February 1945 he was posted to the Air Ministry and survived the war (WMHM Dods Collection)

13th January 1945

Saturday was viewed with suspicion being the thirteenth day of the month. A battle order was announced. The first thing we looked at in the main briefing room was the large map of Europe. The target was the railway yards at Saarbrucken in the Saar basin, south western Germany. The weather was bad, but they said it was possible to take-off, though it would deteriorate later. It was very cold, and we added thick woollen socks and a thick woollen high-necked sweater to our battle dress. While waiting to climb into the aircraft we joined the ground crew in their makeshift hut that they had built and fitted out themselves. Most importantly, it had a warm stove.

After a smooth take-off we were orbiting waiting for our followers. We were on our own. Where were they? Suddenly they showed themselves popping up through the cloud and off we flew. There were Lancasters everywhere, 400 on this trip with full bomb loads. The opposition was not as heavy as we expected but still plenty of flak. We bombed the target and wheeled out quickly setting course for home. One hour from home I received a message and had to use my code book to decipher it. We were to be divert to RAF Exeter because of bad weather. The navigator asked me to get a magnetic bearing from Exeter. This add another 1½ hours to the journey with many more Lancasters already in the circuit already. The airfield was small Spitfire station. It became crowded with 25 huge Lancasters.

After an overnight stay and breakfast, we were taken out to our aircraft but had to wait till refuelling was complete. We said our goodbyes to the ground staff. This was their first experience of having all these extra aircraft to look after. Then we were off again. There were crowds of people watching the take-off. They had never seen so many Lancasters together; just think, though, of the Germans watching 400 passing overhead. After landing at base, we were interrogated and released. That evening a battle order was pinned up.

15th January 1945
This was another visit to the Ruhr: Lagendreer. The target was a coking plant and railway yards. We were ready to go when it was put off for three hours, so we dozed in the main briefing and time dragged. We were by the aircraft when a van raced up it was delayed once again for an hour. It was 3.30am and bitterly cold so we joined the ground crew in their cosy hut. Then, at last, we were off. An uneventful trip with the usual flak etc.

16th January 1945
We were on again for a night operation to Wanne-Eickel oil plants in the Ruhr. The flak was extremely heavy and were glad to drop our load and get out of it. Nights were frightening, and tension mounted as each crew was in a large black world of their own.

20th January 1945
Nothing having happened for three days, we had to fly to Manston with a passenger crew who were to fly back a Lancaster that had made an emergency landing there. When we arrived at Manston our own aircraft broke down, so we had to leave our aircraft at Manston and fly back as passengers in the other plane. What a fiasco!

21st January 1945
Sunday. We did an acceptance test on a new Lancaster.

22nd January 1945
We were briefed for a raid on Duisburg, but it was cancelled. Later we were briefed again for the same raid. The target was a steel plant.

Ten minutes after leaving the target we were attacked by an ME 210 fighter. The first I knew of it was when the skipper threw us into a corkscrew and the guns started chattering. The G force that ensued was so great I couldn't move. I just sat there and hung on. The

Luftwaffe Me 210 fighters, one of which tried to spoil Frank's trip to Duisburg (MTW).

skipper continued to twist and turn and guns firing between the aircraft. I became aware of the smell of cordite and my stomach didn't know where I was. We lost him. He probably went after easier prey. We couldn't relax knowing that he was roaming the skies looking for victims. Fifteen minutes later came another fright. A Lancaster had whizzed across in front of us missing us by a whisker. We were a shaken crew. There was little conversation after this. We were relieved to see Waterbeach circuit lights and the PUNDIT flashing the red WJ letters. Our bodies started to relax when we reached our dispersal point.

Six days leave followed. It passed quickly, and it was soon time to leave Darlington for base. Three days passed hanging around then a battle order was posted.

10th February 1945
We set off for Hohenbudberg on the Ruhr. The target was railway yards. We were back at base. After de-briefing I spent the rest of the day in bed.

13th February 1945

Tuesday February 13th was different somehow. You felt it in the air. We knew something was brewing though nothing had been officially announced. Even when I went out to the dispersals to check our aircraft they seemed to be fevered activity all around. No sooner had I returned to the mess when a battle order was announced.

Flying meal 1700 hours, pre-briefing 1745 hours, main briefing 1830 hours, transport 2040 hours, taxi out 21 hours, first take-off 2110 hours. Even at the Signals briefing things seemed more vital even though the target wasn't mentioned by name. Pop Oulton said this was a big one. We couldn't wait to get into the main briefing room to find out the target. On this trip our crew were designated to be one of the six wind-finders for 3 Group. This was more work for our navigator and me. He had to find the wind speed and direction at our height to fly 21,000 feet every half hour and then I had to transmit it in code back to our own HF/DF station at Waterbeach. It would be passed on to Flying Control and Intelligence, then into Group H.Q. and Bomber Command H.Q. There the mean wind speed received from these crews would be calculated and then transmitted on the next scheduled Bomber Command broadcast to all the main force and like the group forecasts it was transmitted on a Swat/Swab? / transmitter so no operator should miss it. The call sign was A72 on frequency 3050Kc/s. All main force navigators had to use these wind speeds and consequently uniformity in navigation and timing would ensue. That was the logical conclusion in theory, but it was seldom 100%.

In the briefing room all eyes went to the map. We looked at the red tape legs goggle-eyed. What a distance! There were three long legs and one short-legged run to the target, which was in the south east corner of Germany, 120 miles south of Berlin, but a little further east Dresden was the target. Then there were three long legs back to base. At our table the navigator had all his maps and charts plotting the route, identifying all the heavily defended places we had to avoid but you couldn't miss them all. The briefing began. We were told the raid would be in two waves. The first was actually going on as he spoke and due to bomb at 2130 hours. Just as we took off the first wave would be returning. This would be the longest trip so far; nine hours flying. We were told the raid was to help the Russian advance. Each pilot was given a Union Jack to tie round his waist under his clothes. If a crew was shot down they were to press on to the Russian lines and show the Union Jack to show you were English and hope they wouldn't shoot you.

Dresden, we were told, was filled with German troops coming and going to the eastern front. There were also armament works and aircraft component factories. The first wave comprised 300 Lancasters and the second, ours, 500 Lancasters. They would also be an American force of B17s later in the day. We would be carrying a maximum fuel load and a slightly reduced bomb load to compensate. Each Lancaster would be carrying a 4000-lb blockbuster and 8 or 10 500 lb bombs.

There would be a Master Bomber and a force of pathfinders on both raids though they may be surplus to requirements on the second raid. They would also be a number two Master Bomber in case the first was shot down.

The Master of Ceremonies circled the target continuously at a lower height than us, directing the pathfinders' I.T.s and marker flares, and also advising and informing the main force which colours to bomb, whether to advance bombing or retard it. The master bomber could be flying in a Lancaster or a Mosquito from heights of 4,000 to 10,000 feet while the main force would be up above at 21,000 feet. If there was low cloud he would have to drop below the cloud. All his directions came over the vhf radio transmitter.

We were given a fairly new Lancaster to fly that day, D for Dog. There was an unusual atmosphere that day. Rarely had two such forces been sent to share a target. It seemed they meant to do maximum damage. We were concerned that with the first wave over the target all the defences and fighters would be alert and would also have plenty of time to land and refuel before we arrived, so would be ready for us. The camp was in complete lock down all day. The trip to Dresden would be our 26th. We had just been told that instead of doing thirty operations, we now had to do forty, so we still had fourteen more operations to fly.

At last we were ready. Two of the ground crew were in front of us guiding us on to the perimeter track with torches. Now we were on our own with the track only lit by the sparsely scattered blue lights. A sharp lookout had to be kept for wing navigation lights of other aircraft taxiing round to the runway.

We were airborne. The first wave would be on its way back now. We crossed the French coast. I was now very busy with transmissions It would take over four hours to reach Dresden. About an hour from time on target we could see a glow in the distance. At first we didn't associate with the but after another twenty minutes we knew it was Dresden. With half an hour to go we were mesmerised by the huge glow that presented itself to us. We couldn't believe it. It was a holocaust. The city was ablaze. Nobody could be alive down there and we had to add to it.

I switched over to crew intercom and heard the Master Bomber directing us to where to bomb, which colour flares or T. I.s to aim for. It looked like hell down there and I MEAN hell. It's a night I don't think I will ever forget. We dropped our bomb load; a 4,000-lb blockbuster and eight 500 lb bombs. Multiply that 500 times. After allowing the automatic camera time to take its battery of photographs we swung out of that glare. If there were any enemy fighters above us we were silhouetted for them and sitting ducks. There was a little flak, but ground defences must have been saturated. After a half-hour's flying from Dresden we could still see that glare.

However, we were still a long way from home and must be ever alert. As we flew on the roaring of the Merlin engines was comforting and very reassuring. We were now flying at 18,000 feet and would keep that height till we reached the Dutch coast, then lose height a little more quickly. Even though we were at oxygen height it was nice to have a cup of coffee and sandwich though it was a bit difficult getting it under the mask. It didn't seem long before we were approaching the coast. IFF had been switched on earlier. This was the 'Identification Friend or Foe' transmitter which gave out a certain kind of signal which informed the defences we were friendly aircraft. We were approaching base and I could see Pundit, those flashing red letters. We landed at 0615 hrs. We had been flying 9hrs 5mins. We were tired. As usual the ground crew were waiting for us. Some Flying Control staff stepped out on to the veranda and gave us the thumbs up. We were de-briefed. Still etched in our minds was the sight of that city burning. It was devastating. We went to the mess for our eggs and bacon and noticed the battle order pinned up for tomorrow. The next morning at breakfast we heard one crew had not returned from Dresden.

14th February 1945
In the main briefing room, the map was unveiled. The target was Chemnitz. It was thirty miles west of Dresden, another long trip. Once again it was to help the Russian army. It was full of German troops resting. Our aim was to annihilate the German troops.

Once again there was to be a Master Bomber and his deputy plus pathfinders. The weather was clear over Europe and once again the captains wore Union Jacks under their clothes to identify themselves to the Russians. Just one raid with 400 Lancasters. We were told another raid would be going on at the same time at Mannheim. Numbers 4 and 6 Groups, consisting of Lancasters and Halifaxes, would take care of that. We took off in good order.

When we crossed the Belgium coast the searchlights and flak started. A little to the north we saw a huge flash and explosion. Someone had taken a direct hit. We saw tracers across the sky and knew some poor devil was taking it from an enemy fighter. We were worried about enemy fighters being around after yesterday's raid on Dresden, so we were glad when we heard the bomb aimer say, 'Bombs away'. We wheeled around and flew like the clappers till we were well away and settled down to cruising speed. We were fifteen minutes from Waterbeach when the Captain got in touch with base by radio transmitter and was immediately told 'BANDITS'. We were given a heading to fly in the direction of Tempsford and told to orbit there for a while. We soon saw Tempsford Pundit flashing, but at the same time we were told to return to base. It was all clear. This happened now and again at night. The German fighters would infiltrate the bomber stream and fly along with them and play havoc when they reached the airfield. It was pitch black flying at night and couldn't see what was happening. That was why IFF was so

Bridges over the Rhine at Wesel. Frank and his colleagues obliterated the town, meaning that the Allies were able to take it with very few casualties (WMHM).

useful. After a rest and a visit to Cambridge I returned to the mess to find a battle order for the next day.

15th February 1945
The target was Wesel. We were to obliterate the town. This was a support attack. The British army was only five miles away, so our bombing had to be accurate and if in any doubt not to bomb. We heard the British army took Wesel with few casualties. We had no battle orders for the next few days and just went to lectures, practice etc around the base.

20th February 1945
Heard I had been made up to Flight Sergeant.

23rd February 1945

A battle order was pinned on the notice board. Being a daylight raid we were a GH leader. The target was oil plants at Gelsenkirchen in the Ruhr and they were heavily defended. The weather was clear, and everything was going smoothly. We knew we were getting close the flak was terrific and frighteningly so. Then it was 'Bombs away' and we soared away with our followers close behind. We were losing height, down to 10,000 feet, when the message came in. We were to be diverted because of atrocious weather conditions. The cloud base over East Anglia was down to 500 feet. We headed north to Acklington D/F station and asked for a magnetic reading to reach them. We reached Acklington to find four other Lancasters in the circuit. By the time we landed we had been airborne seven hours.

24th February 1945

We returned to base. But before we set course the skipper said he knew I was from Darlington that wasn't far away, and we would 'shoot 'the town which meant fly low. I warned him of the cooling towers. He was as good as his word. I don't think it would have bothered the residents. They were used to aircraft flying over the town on their approach to Middleton St. George airfield.

25th February 1945

Sunday was a routine day checking the aircraft equipment, carrying out routine duties and relaxing.

26th February 1945

It started off as another lazy day. We were perplexed by the inaction. Then a battle order was announced for the next day, so it was early to bed.

27th February 1945

It was an early take-off. We were airborne at 0730 hours. We were in G for George. The target was Gelsenkirchen again. This time we were aiming for a coking plant. The flak was terrific on the last leg in. Just before commencing the run in I saw a Lancaster receive a direct hit. It must have been a wing because it went down in flames and then exploded. We arrived back safely. This was our 31st operation. That evening another battle order was announced. Another early night and call for 0400 hours.

28th February 1945

It was Gelsenkirchen again. The intention was the annihilation of German troops. We took off, picked up our followers and set course. We felt reassured when we saw our fighter escort above us. I took a look out of the astrodome. There were 700 Lancasters on this trip and what a sight they made, disappearing into specks ahead of us and behind us. Aircraft were gently undulating in the air currents from the propellers. I could see the mid-upper and rear gunner turrets moving round searching the sky, watching for the unexpected.

Suddenly the flak started. There was no information from Bomber Command broadcasts. Soon we were on the bombing run. Flak was coming in thick and fast and aircraft weaving all over the place. I could see Lancasters coming up behind us. I was just praying we could bomb and get away before they came above us on their bombing run. No snags. As soon as the bomb aimer said OK, we swung away and flew like a bat out of hell away from the target. The flak was being hurled up more than ever now. The German gunners below appeared to be obsessed with flinging shells up as fast as they could. It was terrific and terrifying believe me. To get more speed Hendy put the nose down a little losing a little height but a fast getaway from the area. We reduced to cruising speed and began to lose height a little. We were now over allied occupied Europe. Flak was no longer a problem, but enemy aircraft were. We were now at 10,000 feet. It was good to take-off the oxygen mask of my face and out came the coffee flasks. After we crossed the Dutch coast I switched on IFF for our ground radar to recognise us as friendly aircraft as we approached the English coastline. Soon we were in de-briefing. After a wash and brush up went into Cambridge to the Regal cinema to unwind.

1st March 1945

There was an ENSA show on so we all went to see it.

2nd March 1945

Friday morning, the tannoy announced a battle order. Today it was Cologne and it was impressed upon us unless we were dead sure we were not to bomb but to bring our bombs back. Apparently, the weather was bad over the target. It was going to be solid cloud all over Europe and the base only 3,000 feet. So it turned out we brought our load back, but not before I had the fright of my life. We were actually on the bombing run with the bomb doors open. The ack-ack was coming up thick and fast and I was in the astrodome watching our two followers, then suddenly three Lancasters in V formation also on their bombing run were right above us with their bomb doors open. Seeing the blockbuster and the other 1000 lb bombs hanging above us waiting to be release made me freeze for a moment then I yelled to the pilot over the intercom to move to port quickly. Danger was averted. Then I heard the pilot say to the bomb aimer that we weren't bombing and to close the bomb doors. Our followers closed their bomb doors and we headed home.

5th March 1945

Another battle order was posted. Call up 0400 hours. The target today was Salzbergen, an oil plant. The flight, bombing and return followed the same pattern with the same hazards, with heavy flak from a heavily defended plant.

7th March 1945

Wednesday dawned bright and beautiful. We wondered what they would have for us today. We didn't have long to wait. At 1000 hours we were on another battle order. A night trip and a long one. We were going to Dessau somewhere near Leipzig, but the route consisted of a larger number of legs to try and fool the Germans. The target was to obliterate the town.

1710 hours we were airborne. Somehow, probably owing to difference in wind speed forecast and actual wind speed, on the leg before the final run in leg to Dessau we were well off course and passed over Magdeburg, and didn't we get a pasting. It was like Guy Fawkes Night. But we got there even though there was damage to the rudder. We dropped our bombs and flew home a weary shaken crew. This was the longest trip yet, at 9 hours 20 minutes.

10th March 1945
We were up bright and early 0715 hours.
Target Gelsenkirchen again!!! This time to the oil plants. Could there be any left? We knew it would be no pushover being in the Ruhr. It was known the Germans were in desperate need for oil, so it would be heavily defended. It turned out to be an ordinary run. Just the expected amount of flak hurled up at us. We were back at 1735 hours. In the evening a dance had been arranged in the Officers Mess. We went down to join in, but we were too tired and left early for bed.

11th March 1945
Sunday brought us back to life. The weather was terrible, gale force winds tearing about. There would be no flights today, so I went to the camp cinema. That night a battle order was pinned up for the next day. Breakfast would be 0700hours.

12th March 1945
After pre-op formalities were over we assembled in the main briefing room. The target was Dortmund in the Ruhr. This one was going to be a big one and a better target. There would be 1030 Lancasters and Halifaxes, 40 Mosquitos and a fighter escort of Mustangs and Spitfires. The sky was going to be crowded. The raid had been planned meticulously. Everyone to keep to their heights etc. The weather was going to be fine all day. Dortmund wouldn't know what hit them. The Americans were sending 200 bombers to Munich at about the same time. 30 Lancasters were going from Waterbeach. The roar of those Merlin engines, some idling was terrific. There was always an audience for such a take-off. Our two followers soon found us, and we started to gain height. Ten minutes later we set course. We were in the first wave. Our fighter escort picked us up over the North Sea Just before we reached the Dutch coast the fighters would climb to 30,000 feet ready to swoop down on enemy fighters. Looking out of the astrodome for a moment I had never seen so many four-engine aircraft on a raid before. We had flak from time to time en-route. I noticed in the distance the

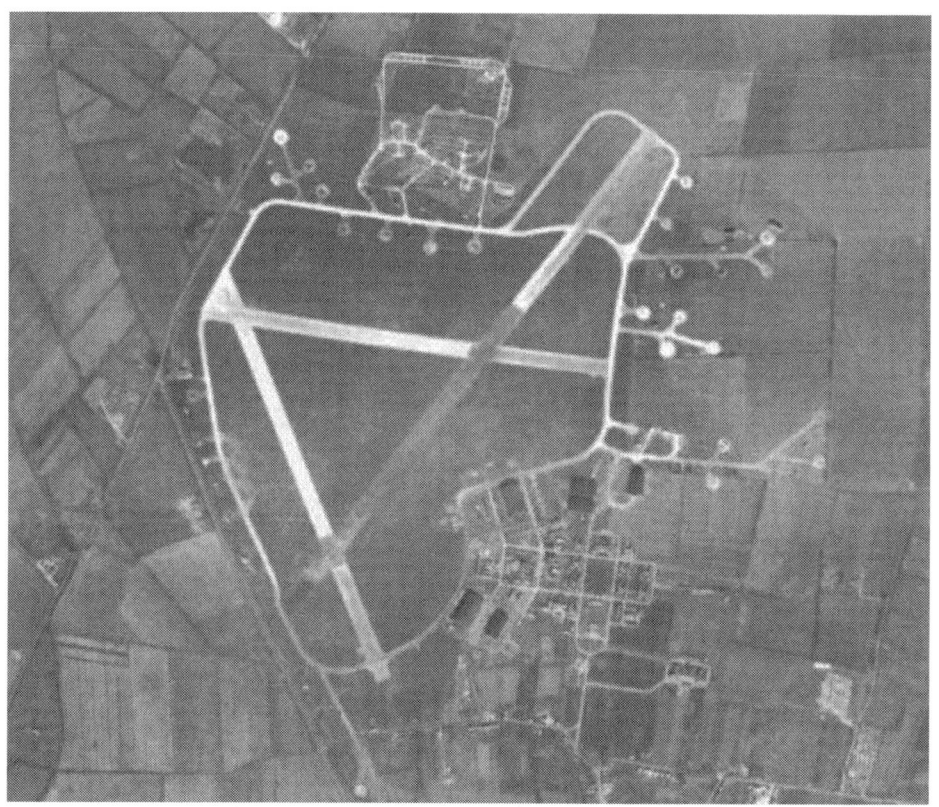
A bird's eye view of RAF Waterbeach in 1945 (WMHM).

white vertical vapour trails of the launch of a V2 rocket. A few more minutes and that would land on London.

In another half hour we would be approaching Dortmund and what a surprise they were going to get. I got into the astrodome to start observing and plugged into the intercom our two followers were still close. We were in the clear. No one too close. We were now on our bombing run. Flak was thick and furious. One Lancaster away on the port side was ablaze and I noticed another with an engine feathered and smoke coming from it. With luck he might get back. Everything went according to plan. We dropped our load of bombs, swung away from the target and flak and set off for home. Approaching England there were Lancasters and Halifaxes everywhere heading to their respective bases such as Methwold, Mildenhall, Tuddenham, Ockington, Bourn, Gravely, Lakenheath, Masham, Newmarket, Downham Market, Mepal,

77

Witchford and others. We were first back at Waterbeach. The first time we had that honour. The flight took 5 hours 50 minutes. After a quick inspection there didn't seem to be any damage. At the de-briefing we reported the plight of the two Lancasters and the V2 rocket and its approximate launch position. Someone would shortly be paying a visit to the site.

13th March 1945

I rode to our aircraft to check the equipment. The armourers were bombing up. It was a hive of activity. Something was to come off. Sure enough a battle order was out. Halfway through the briefing it was cancelled. We were to go to Hattingen. The target was an oil plant.

14th March 1945

We were briefed for the same flight and took off at 1300 hours. The trip was uneventful except from all the usual hazards such as flak and ack-ack.

Unfortunately, on this raid a friend of mine was killed. He was also a wireless operator / air gunner[3]. Sadly, he was the only one killed in the aircraft. He was in the astrodome when flak shrapnel took off the astrodome and his head. It was a terrible shock. We notice the ambulance following the Lancaster round the perimeter to a nearby dispersal. We all went to see what had happened (not knowing at that time what had happened). It was a terrible shock. We saw the absence of the astrodome and part of the rear cockpit canopy, but they made it home. Everyone concerned was distraught.

15th March 1945

We went on six days leave. I returned to Darlington. On return to base we hung around for days.

26th March 1945

A battle order was announced for the next day. Flying meal for 0615 hours so we had an early night.

---

[3] *Flight Sergeant William Sparkes was the wireless operator for the crew of Acting Squadron Leader Keith Cendick commander of A Flight. He was on his 32nd operation.*

27ᵗʰ March 1945

In the main briefing room all eyes were on the map. The red tapes stretched to the northern part of the Ruhr. The target was Hamm. We knew it was heavily defended especially by flak. It was a very busy marshalling yard. It was to be completely destroyed and consequently nearby Hamm would be battered. The mission was uneventful except for the usual hazards. The days that followed were spent on routine activities.

1ˢᵗ April 1945

A raid was laid on for Stuttgart, then scrubbed.

4ᵗʰ April 1945

After lunch a battle order was announced for a night operation. This was to be our last operation. The target was to synthetic oil plants at Merseburg, near Leipzig, a fairly long trip. It was heavily defended. After briefing everyone came to wish us well on our last operation. Even the C.O. 514 squadron came to wish us well. We were flying in F for Freddy tonight. After we crossed the Dutch coast there were four legs to the target and three back. Flak was spasmodic at various points. It seemed an unusually long trip but at last we were nearing the last before turning on to the bombing run. The bomb doors would be open. We were so vulnerable. I heard the master gunner on the radio transmitter giving corrections for the main force, which colour T.I.s to aim for and which to ignore. T.I. s were Target Identification flares. With a deep sigh of relief, I heard Pat say, 'Bombs away' for the last time. Another couple of minutes for the camera to do its work then we were wheeling away out of the target area as fast as we could go. I drew back the curtain for a glimpse out. It looked like hell let loose. Three types of coloured flares were falling towards the target red, yellow and green. Search lights were tracing all over the sky including two blue radar controlled searchlights. The flak bursts showed deep red and yellowish. White flares were falling from above which meant fighters were up there looking for us, waiting to pounce.

After we bombed, the few minutes waiting for the camera to get its battery of pictures seemed an age. A further five minutes flying, and we were well away from the glare of lights and target area. Now the time to look for enemy fighters. This was the time when they were most active and determined to press home attacks. I closed the curtain and turned up my little lamp light I was allowed to work with. With just an hour to go we were crossing the Dutch coast at 12,000 feet. We crossed the English coast at Aldeburgh and reeled in the training aerial for the last time. Twenty minutes later we joined the circuit. Control congratulated us over the air for successfully finishing our tour of duty of 40 operations.

Everyone was congratulating us. It was very emotional. After a night out with all our friends we would be leaving Waterbeach and never see them again. We were debriefed. Congratulations continued to flow and much hand shaking including the various Commanding Officers and Intelligence. At last we went for our last flying breakfast and were given two eggs instead of one in honour of the occasion. The next night we had our celebrations. There were 15 of us – and what a celebration. Saturday and Sunday were spent clearing up before going on leave for 14 days. We were to return to Waterbeach when we would find out what was to happen to us next.

Second Time Around

23rd April 1945

I returned from leave and spent the next few days helping in the Signals section. I was then sent to Catterick for various tests and assessments. I was eventually sent to Homesley South. I discovered this was a Transport Command Station. My role was now reversed. I was now ground crew. The work was varied including the repatriation of Canadian airmen. By August I was working full time at HD/FD station. In my off-duty time I was able to explore the country in the county and along the south coast. I was now a Warrant Officer. I was demobbed in December 1946 and given 56 days determination leave.

Christmas and New Year came and went, and I still hadn't decided what I wanted to do with my life. Then I received a letter from RAF Records Office suggesting if I hadn't decided what to do, would I consider going back into the RAF. They wanted me back as air crew, but I could go in as ground crew if I preferred. I didn't need to think twice and accepted the offer to go into aircrew.

In August I reported to Burton Wood and was sworn in again. I found myself taking various courses and became a staff wireless operator instructor. In October I was posted to Driffield, Yorkshire and two month later transferred to Middleton-St.-George near Darlington. We were doing local flying in Wellingtons and Ansons and flying as staff wireless operator with pupil trainee wireless operators. The Wellingtons were taken out of service in 1948. Out of the blue I was posted on loan to No. 21 Group Headquarters near Lincoln for 6 weeks and then returned to Middleton-St.-George.

Authors' note: Here the notes stopped in February 1948.

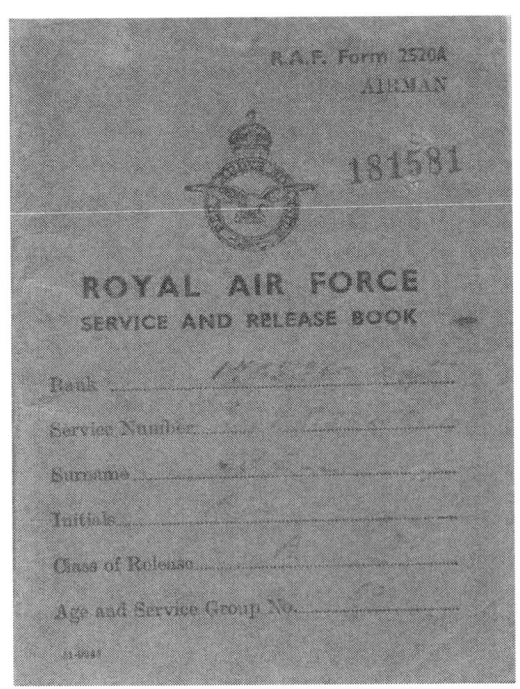

Frank's Service and Release Book from the RAF. He left as a Warrant Officer, the most senior NCO rank.

Frank's war medals. Left to right: The 1939-45 Star, the France and Germany Star, the 1939-45 War Medal.

Reunions

The 514 Squadron Association has successfully run reunions for many years, this tradition continuing to the time of publication. The events provide an opportunity for old comrades to get together at Waterbeach, and for family and friends to commemorate their duty and, in so many cases, their sacrifice.

Above: In 1947 the first 514 Squadron reunion took place. Frank Bell is number 4 in the photo; number 3 is his former CO, Wing Commander Mike Wyatt DFC. Below: the annual reunion of 514 Squadron is always a convivial occasion. Frank took these photos at one such event; unfortunately, he did not make a note of which of his former comrades are pictured.

Epilogue: The Mynarski Memorial Commemoration, 28th August 2014

For two months in 2014, the only two airworthy Lancasters in the world operated a series of flights over the UK. The RAF's PA474, KC-A 'Thumper III' was joined by the Canadian Warplane Heritage Museum's Mk. X Lancaster, serial number KB726, coded VR-A and popularly known as 'Vera'.

Royal Canadian Airforce officer Andrew Mynarski, to whom the Canadian Lancaster is dedicated, died trying to rescue a colleague after their plane was shot down. Frank's sons were fortunate to secure tickets for the event. They took him to Durham Tees Valley Airport to see the Andrew Mynarski Memorial Lancaster touch down.

Mynarski has a statue at his wartime base at the airport which was formerly Royal Canadian Airforce and RAF station, RAF Middleton-St.-George,

These photographs are from that memorable day. As a Bomber Command veteran, Frank was treated like a VIP. The captain was most kind helping Frank into the aircraft to recapture the feelings of past times and talking about his memories.

The Canadian Lancaster was a very popular visitor to the former RAF and RCAF station, providing an opportunity for the public to get a close look at this iconic aircraft.

Frank at Middleton St. George with friends, including Vera. **Left to right:** *Ken Bell, unnamed veteran, Frank Bell, Andrew Bell.*

Above left: Visitors explore the cavernous bomb bay of the Lancaster. The step ladder would not normally have formed part of the bomb load.

Above right: Frank is presented with a copy of the 514 Squadron War Diary, 'Striking Through Clouds', by author and squadron historian Simon Hepworth.

Left: Frank with a fellow veteran, believed to have served with 44 (Rhodesia) Squadron, along with Bomber Command re-enactors. Opposite page top: Re-enactors pose in front of the Mynarski Memorial.

Bottom: Frank on board 'Vera' with a member of the Canadian crew. Veterans were, rightly, treated as heroes.

Waterbeach Today

After the war, RAF Waterbeach remained in the hands of the Ministry of Defence for many decades. Bomber Command passed the station to Fighter Command in 1950, the airfield hosting Meteor, Javelin and Hunter jet fighters until in 1963 it became the base for the Airfield Construction Branch. Subsequently it fell into the hands of the Army, becoming the home of the Royal Engineers. Popularly known as 'The Beach', it is fondly remembered by a large number of service personnel who served there.

Above: Frank and friends outside the Watch Office at Waterbeach.
Below: The tank gives away the fact that the Army is now in residence.

Two of the remaining hangars from the wartime era. They were still standing proudly on the airfield in 2017.

Appendix 1: Wireless Operator's Log

WIRELESS OPERATORS (AIR) LOG

SQUADRON * 1 H.N.S.	AIRCRAFT NH 457	DATE 2?-11- 47
CAPTAIN F/LT. BENSON	NAVIGATOR N? ??????	WIRELESS OP. SIG.? BELL
AIRBORNE 1038	NATURE OF FLIGHT * X. COUNTRY	LANDED 1239

N.F.T. (OR D.I.)			AFTER FLIGHT CHECK			
ITEM	S. OR U/S	INITIALS	ITEM		S OR U/S	INITIALS
INTER COMM.	S		INTER COMM.	OFF	?	
W/T TRANSMITTER	S		W/T TRANSMITTER	OFF	S	
W/T RECEIVER	S	JB	W/T RECEIVER	OFF	S	JB
R/T SET	S		R/T SET	OFF	S	
I.F.F.	/		I.F.F.	OFF	/	
W/T SPARES	S		W/T SPARES		S	

CAPTAINS REMARKS (AFTER FLIGHT)

S.B.A	OK	R/T	OK	INTER. COMM.	OK	SIGNATURE ?????, F/L

INFORMATION

OPERATIONAL CALL SIGN:	MNPPG	STATION R/T AIRCRAFT CALL SIGN:	DUSTCAP 'C'
BASE COLLECTIVE CALL SIGN:	MNPPC̄	SQUADRON R/T AIRCRAFT CALL SIGN:	DRIFFIELD)
GROUP COLLECTIVE CALL SIGN:	MPBJC̄		TOWER)

"TINSEL" FREQUENCIES: CEASE JAMMING:

M.F. D/F SECTION(S) ALLOTTED: " C " 440 Kc/s MQF.

BASIC Q.F.E.   1009

W/T CONTACT STN. — HV - HULLAVINGTON. & 9FG. (GROUP)

FLIGHT PLAN

POSITION	E.T.A.	FACILITIES AVAILABLE & ACTION
1 LEG	80	BASE - LINDHOLME - SWINDERBY - SYERSTON -
		SHAWBURY - DEFFORD - HULLAVINGTON.
2 LEG	35	HULLAVINGTON - WYMESWOLDE - CALSHOT
3 LEG	70	WATTON - WYMESWOLDE - SYERSTON -
		SWINDERBY
QTE's		SEALAND - ACKLINGTON - BIRCHAM NEWTON.
		M/F BEACONS.
1 LEG.		LYNEHAM - NORTHOLT
2 LEG		HORSHAM ST. FAITH
3 LEG		BINBROOK

* SQUADRON & NATURE OF FLIGHT TO BE ENTERED AFTER LANDING

91

TIME	CALL	SIGNS	TEXT, ACTION, BEARINGS, FIXES, ETC.	T.O.O.	I.F.F	VOLTS	PORT AMP	STBD AMP
1036			ON WATCH 7Bell					
38			AIRBORNE					
39			METER READINGS			28		
40			OVER TO GØL (Driffield control)					
	GØL	MNPPG	ØRV ? ØOP K					
	G	GØL	R- ØOP 1 =	10412				
	GØL	G	R+					
			PILOT INFORMED					
43			OVER TO DR (Driffield D/F)					
	DR	MNPPG	? ØOP ? ØSA K					
	G	DR	R- ØOP 1 - ØSA 5 K					
44	DR	G	R +					
47			TRAILING AERIAL OUT					
48			OVER TO LB (Lindholme)					
	LB	MNPPG	? ØDM K					
	G	LB	R K					
	LB	G	R —					
	G	LB	R - ØDM 170- 3G =	10502				
51	LB	G	R+					
53			OVER TO SØ (Swindered)					
	SØ	MNPPG	? ØDM K					
	G	SØ	R K					
	SØ	G	R —					
	G	SØ	R - ØDM 085- 3G =	10552				
	SØ	G	R+					
59			OVER TO YFG					
		YFG	- 7- vvv ØTT -	11032				
1104			METER READINGS			28		
05			OVER TO GØL					
	GØL	MNPPG	ØTC K					
	G	GØL	R K					
	GØL	G	- P- GR 5- BK - A- PN - 5305N 0251W =	11003				

TIME	CALL	SIGNS	TEXT, ACTION, BEARINGS, FIXES, ETC.	T.O.O.	I.F.F	VOLTS	AMP	AMP
1105	G	GΦ1	R+					
09			OVER TO SY (Shawbury)					
	SY	MNPPG	? ΦDM k					
	G	SY	R K					
	SY	G	R —					
	G	SY	R - ΦDM 277 - 3G =	1102				
11	SY	G	R+					
22			OVER TO DF HV (Hullavington)					
	HV	MNPPG	? ΦDM k					
	G	HV	R K					
	HV	G	R —					
	G	HV	R - ΦDM 104 - 3B ≈	1124Z				
25	HV	G	R+					
29			OVER TO 9FG					
		9FG	- 9 - vvv ΦYT -	1132Z				
34			METER READINGS		28			
35	9FG	MNPPG	? ΦΦV GΦ1 k					
	G	9FG	R - K					
	9FG	G	- P-T- B - MNPPG - GΦ1 - GR5 =					
			BKO - A - PN - 5240N 0240W ×	1133Z				
39	G	9FG	R+					
40			OVER TO DF (Defford)					
	DF	MNPPG	? ΦDM k					
	G	DF	R K					
	DF	G	R -					
	G	DF	R - ΦDM 240 - 3G =	1143Z				
44	DF	G	R+					
47			OVER TO MΦF (Sealand) (control)					
	MΦF	MNPPG	? ΦTE k					
	G	MΦF	R K					
	MΦF	G	R —					
	G	MΦF	ΦTE - 172 - 1 =	1149				
51	MΦF	G	R+					

TIME	CALL SIGNS		TEXT, ACTION, BEARINGS, FIXES, ETC.	T. O. O.	I.P.F.	VOLTS	PORT AMP.	T.B.D AMP.
1200			OVER TO 9F9					
		9F9	-1- ··· P4T-	12032				
04			METER READINGS			28		
04			OVER TO 9Φ1					
	9Φ1	MNPP9	ΦTC K					
	9	9Φ1	R K					
	9Φ1	9	-P- 9R5=BK0-A-P̄N̄ - 5345N					
			0010W =	12002				
11	9	9Φ1	R +					
15			OVER TO MΦF					
	MΦF	MNPP9	? ΦTF K					
	9	MΦF	R K					
	MΦF	9	R —					
	9	MΦF	ΦTF 5358N 0006W =	12182				
19	MΦF	9	R +					
20			OVER TO SJ (Syerton					
	SJ	MNPP9	? ΦDM K					
	9	SJ	R K					
	SJ	9	R —					
	9	SJ	R- ΦDM 098 - 39=	12232				
24	SJ	9	R +					
25			OVER TO 9Φ1					
	9Φ1	MNPP9	ΦTC K					
	9	9Φ1	R K					
	9Φ1	9	ΦAA 9Φ1- 12402- ? ΦPW K					
27	9	9Φ1	R- ĀS̄					
29	9	9Φ1	R- ΦPW K					
	9Φ1	9	R +					
31			OVER ON TO VHF					
39			LANDED					
40			OFF WATCH J.Bell					

94

Appendix 2: List of Frank Bell's Operations

Frank's usual crew was as follows, except as stated under 'Crew Changes' in the following table of operations:

F/Lt. Fred. Hendy, pilot.
Sgt Ernie Wall, flight engineer.
P/O Rob Simons, navigator.
P/O Pat Jackson, bomb aimer.
F/Sgt Frank Bell, WOP/AG.
W/O George Sales, mid-upper gunner.
Sgt Taffy Harris, rear gunner.

Date	D/N	A/C Type	Serial	Code	Target	Bombing Height	ORB Notes	Crew changes
05/11/1944	D	Lancaster I	NG142	A2-H	Solingen	17,500	Bomb load 1 x 4000 HC, 6 x 1000 ANM59, 4 x 500 GP, 2 x 500 GP (L/Delay). Primary target: Solingen. Weather 10/10ths cloud over target. Bombed at 13.04 hours from 17,500 feet on leading aircraft.	MUG Sgt Harris. RG Sgt Tranter
11/11/1944	D	Lancaster I	PD324	A2-B	Castrop Rauxel	19,000	Bomb load 1 x 4000 HC. 16 x 500 GP. Primary target: Castrop Rauxel, Oil refineries. Weather 10/10ths cloud. Bombed at 11.07 hours from 19,000 feet on G.H. Leader.	MUG Sgt Sharvin
16/11/1944	D	Lancaster I	PD324	A2-B	Heinsburg	9,000	Bomb load 1 x 4000 HC, 6 x 1000 MC, 6 x 500 GP. Primary target: Heinsburg. Weather - nil cloud with slight haze over target. Bombed at 15.31½ hours from 9,000 feet. Church - Master Bomber said don't bomb T.I.s.	MUG Sgt Sharvin
20/11/1944	D	Lancaster I	PD334	A2-D	Homberg	20,000	Bomb load 1 x 4000 HC, 3 x 500 GP, 13 x 500 MC. Primary target: Homberg. Weather 10/10ths cloud over target. Bombed at 15.14 hours from 20,000 feet on G.H. Leader.	MUG Sgt Sharvin
23/11/1944	D	Lancaster I	PD325	A2-L	Nordstern (Gelsenkirchen)	20,000	Bomb load 1 x 4000 HC. 16 x 500 GP. Primary target: Nordstern, Gelsenkirchen Oil refineries. Weather 10/10ths cloud. Bombed at 15:23 hours from 20,000 feet with leading aircraft and Red flares.	MUG Sgt Clarke
27/11/1944	D	Lancaster I	PD325	A2-L	Cologne	20,000	Bomb load 1 x 4000 HC, 16 x 500 GP. Primary target: Cologne, Marshalling Yards. Weather patchy cloud. Bombed at 15.05½ hours from 20,000 feet with G.H. Leader.	MUG Sgt Clarke

Date	D/N	Aircraft	Serial	Code	Target	Altitude	Remarks	Crew
29/11/1944	D	Lancaster I	PD325	A2-L	Neuss	20,000	Bomb load 1 x 4000 HC, 6 x 1000 MC, 6 x 500 GP, 3 Flares Red/Green flares. Primary target: Neuss. Weather 10/10ths cloud over target but the glow of fires was seen through cloud. Bombed at 05.38 hours from 20,000 feet. Red flares with Green stars. T.I.s very well concentrated.	MUG Sgt Clarke
04/12/1944	D	Lancaster I	PD334	A2-D	Oberhausen	20,000	Bomb load 1 x 4000 HC, 6 x 1000 MC, 6 x 500 GP. Primary target: Oberhausen, Built up area. Weather 10/10ths cloud. Bombed at 14.08½ hours from 20,000 feet on release of G.H. Leader.	MUG Sgt Clarke
05/12/1944	D	Lancaster I	PD334	A2-D	Hamm	20,000	Bomb load 1 x 4000 HC, 14 x 500 GP, 2 x 500 GP Long Delay. Primary target: Hamm. Weather 10/10ths cloud over target, but otherwise varying from 6-10/10ths. Bombed at 11.29½ hours from 20,000 feet on G.H. Leader.	MUG Sgt Clarke
06/12/1944	N	Lancaster I	PD334	A2-D	Merseburg	21,000	Bomb load 1 x 4000 HC, 8 x 500 GP, 1 x 500 GP Long Delay. Primary target: Merseburg. Weather 10/10ths cloud with odd breaks. Bombed at 20.50½ hours from 21,000 feet on upwind edge of flares.	MUG Sgt Clarke
16/12/1944	D	Lancaster III	LM627	A2-H	Siegen	18,000	Bomb load 1 x 4000 HC, 5 x 1000 MC, 7 x 500 GP. Primary target: Siegen. Weather very bad on route with icing and cloud. Bombed at 15.01 hours from 18,000 feet on G.H. Leader.	MUG Sgt Clarke
21/12/1944	D	Lancaster I	NG118	A2-E	Trier	18,000	Bomb load 1 x 4000 HC, 10 x 500 GP, 6 x 250 GP. Primary target: Trier, Marshalling yards. Weather 10/10 cloud, tops 6/9000 feet. Bombed at 15.01 hours from 18,000 feet on G.H.	MUG Sgt Clarke
23/12/1944	D	Lancaster I	NG118	A2-E	Trier	17,000	Bomb load 1 x 4000 HC, 10 x 500 GP, 6 x 250 GP. Primary target: Trier. Weather clear over target. Bombed at 14.33 hours from 17,000 feet on centre of town.	MUG Sgt Clarke

Date	D/N	Aircraft	Serial	Code	Target	Height	Details	Crew
28/12/1944	D	Lancaster I	PA186	A2-G	Cologne Gremberg	19,500	Bomb load 1 x 4000 HC, 10 x 500 GP, 4 x 250 Red T.I.s. Primary target: Koln Gremberg. Marshalling yards. Weather 10/10ths cloud or fog. Bombed at 15.04½ hours from 19,500 feet on G.H.	MUG Sgt Clarke
31/12/1944	D	Lancaster III	PB482	A2-K	Vohwinkle	19,500	Bomb load 1 x 4000 HC, 2 x 500 M58, 10 x 500 M64, 2 x 500 GP, 1 Flare. Primary target: Vohwinkle. Weather 10/10ths cloud on approaching target although the target itself was clear. Bombed at 14.42 hours from 19,500 feet on G.H.	MUG Sgt Clarke
01/01/1945	N	Lancaster III	PB482	A2-K	Vohwinkle	20,500	Bomb load 1 x 4000 HC, 12 x 500 ANM64, 2 x 500 GP. Primary target: Vohwinkle. Weather clear. Bombed at 19.34 hours from 20,500 feet on G.H.	MUG Sgt Clarke
03/01/1945	D	Lancaster I	PA186	A2-G	Dortmund Huckarde	21,000	Bomb load 1 x 4000 HC, 12 x 500 ANM58 or 64. 3 x 500 GP. 1 Flare. Primary target: Dortmund Huckarde. Weather 10/10ths cloud over target. Bombed at 15.32 hours from 21,000 feet on G.H.	MUG Sgt Clarke
05/01/1945	D	Lancaster I	PA186	A2-G	Ludwigshafen	20,000	Bomb load 1 x 4000 HC, 10 x 500 ANM58 or 64. 2 x 500 GP. 1 Flare. Primary target: Ludwigshafen. Marshalling yards. Weather clear over target. Bombed at 15.08 hours from 20,000 feet on G.H. Aircraft hit by flak, fuselage damaged.	MUG Sgt Clarke
06/01/1945	N	Lancaster I	PA186	A2-G	Neuss	19,800	Bomb load 1 x 4000 HC, 10 x 500 ANM64, 4 x 250 Red T.I.s. Primary target: Neuss. Weather 8-10/10ths cloud over target. Bombed at 18.47 hours from 19,800 feet on G.H.	MUG Sgt Clarke
11/01/1945	D	Lancaster III	LM627	A2-H	Krefeld	19,500	Bomb load 1 x 4000 HC, 10 x 500 ANM64. 4 x 250 GP. 1 Flare. Primary target: Krefeld. Weather 10/10ths cloud above and below. Visibility poor. Bombed at 15.11¼ hours from 19,500 feet on G.H.	MUG Sgt Clarke

Date	D/N	Type	Serial	Code	Target	Height	Details	Remarks
13/01/1945	D	Lancaster I	PA186	A2-G	Saarbrucken	19,500	Bomb load 1 x 4000 HC, 10 x 500 ANM58 or 64, 4 x 250 GP. Primary target: Saarbrucken. Weather 3-5/10ths cloud, tops 4/5,000 feet. Bombed at 15.24 hours from 19,500 feet on G.H. All aircraft of this ops were diverted on return to Exeter as weather at base was unfit to land.	MUG Sgt Clarke. 2nd pilot F/O Matkin.
15/01/1945	D	Lancaster I	PA186	A2-G	Lagendreer	19,000	Bomb load 1 x 4000 HC, 10 x 500 ANM64, 4 x 250 GP, 1 Flare. Primary target: Lagendreer. Weather 10/10ths cloud. Bombed at 15.01½ hours from 19,000 feet on G.H.	MUG Sgt Clarke
16/01/1945	N	Lancaster I	PA186	A2-G	Wanne-Eickel	18,000	Bomb load 1 x 4000 HC, 10 x 500 ANM58, 4 x 250 GP, 1 Flare. Primary target: Wanne-Eickel, Benzol plant. Weather 10/10ths thin low cloud. Bombed at 02.27 hours from 18,000 feet on G.H.	MUG Sgt Clarke. 2nd pilot S/L Wilcox.
22/01/1945	N	Lancaster I	PA186	A2-G	Hamborn (Duisburg)	20,000	Bomb load 1 x 4000 HC, 7 x 500 ANM58 or 64, 2 x 500 GP (L/Delay), 3 x 250 GP. Primary target: Hamborn, Thyssen works. Weather over target clear and almost as bright as day. Bombed at 20.08½ hours from 20,000 feet on centre of red T.Is.	MUG Sgt Clarke
08/02/1945	N	Lancaster I	NG203	A2-C	Hohenbudberg	18,300	Bomb load 1 x 4000 HC, 2 x 500 MC, 4 x 250 GP, 4 x 500 GP, 6 x 500 ANM64. Primary target: Hohenbudberg, Marshalling yards. Weather 8/10ths cloud over target. Bombed at 06.26 hours from 18,300 feet on Red T.Is. Large fires seen on target area.	MUG F/S Sales for all subsequent ops. Nav F/O Nye
13/02/1945	N	Lancaster I	PA186	A2-G	Dresden	19,500	Bomb load 1 x 500 MC, 15 x No. 14 Clusters. Primary target: Dresden. Weather 5/10ths cloud over target. Bombed at 01.38½ hours from 19,500 feet on centre of fires.	Nav F/O Nye. 2nd pilot F/O Jones.
14/02/1945	N	Lancaster I	NN776	A2-D	Chemnitz	19,300	Bomb load 1 x 500 MC, 15 x No. 14 Clusters. Primary target: Chemnitz. Weather 8-10/10ths cloud, tops 15-16,000 feet with occasional breaks. Bombed at 00.34 hours from 19,300 feet on Red/Green flares.	

Date	D/N	Aircraft	Serial	Code	Target	Height	Remarks	Notes
16/02/1945	D	Lancaster I	NG298	JI-E	Wesel	20,000	Bomb load 1 x 4000 HC, 4 x 500 GP, 2 x 500 MC L/Delay, 4 x 250 GP, 6 x 500 ANM64. Primary target: Wesel. Weather clear. Bombed at 16.00½ hours from 20,000 feet on centre of built up area.	Nav F/L Jarvis. 2nd pilot P/O Winkworth.
23/02/1945	D	Lancaster I	NN781	A2-D	Gelsenkirchen	20,000	Bomb load 1 x 4000 HC, 9 x 500 ANM64. 2 x 500 MC, 4 x 250 GP. Primary target Gelsenkirchen. Weather 10/10ths cloud. Bombed at 15.00 hours from 20,000 feet on leading aircraft. On return landed at Hutton Cranswick	Nav Sgt Banham for all subsequent ops.
27/02/1945	D	Lancaster I	NG203	A2-C	Gelsenkirchen	20,000	Bomb load 1 x 4000 HC. 2 x 500 MC (L/D 37B), 9 x 500 ANM64. 4 x 250 GP. Primary target: Gelsenkirchen (Alma Pluto) Benzin plant. Weather 10/10ths cloud, 6/10,000 feet tops. Bombed at 14.27 hours from 20,000 feet on G.H. Leader.	
28/02/1945	D	Lancaster I	NG203	A2-C	Nordstern (Gelsenkirchen)	20,100	Bomb load 1 x 4000 HC, 9 x 500 ANM64, 2 x 500 MC L/D, 4 x 250 GP. Primary target: Nordstern (Gelsenkirchen). Weather 10/10ths cloud. Bombed at 12.05½ hours from 20,100 feet on leading aircraft.	
02/03/1945	D	Lancaster I	NN717	A2-E	Koln	x	Bomb load 1 x 4000 HC, 12 x 500 ANM64. Primary target: Koln. Weather 10/10ths cloud over Koln. South and South-East of Koln clear. Abortive sortie. Bomb load brought back to Base.	
06/03/1945	D	Lancaster I	NF966	A2-G	Salzbergen	21,000	Bomb load 1 x 4000 HC, 12 x 500 ANM64, 2x 500MC. Primary target: Salzbergen. Wintershall oil plant. Weather 10/10ths cloud over target, tops 10,000 feet. Bombed at 12.14½ hours from 21,000 feet on leading G.H. aircraft.	
07/03/1945	N	Lancaster I	NF966	A2-G	Dessau	19,500	Bomb load 1 x 4000 HC, 6 x Mk.17 Clusters. Primary target: Dessau. Weather 5 to 10/10ths thin cloud. Bombed at 22.08 hours from 19,500 feet on Red T.Is.	2nd pilot F/L Rice.

					Bomb load 1 x 4000 HC, 13 x 500 ANM64, 2 x 500 MC. Primary target: Gelsenkirchen. Weather 10/10ths cloud at target, tops 8,000 feet. Bombed at 15.37 hours from 19,000 feet on leading G.H. aircraft. Squadron formation good. Attack should be accurate.
10/03/1945	D	Lancaster III	ME529	A2-F	Gelsenkirchen	19,000	
					Bomb load 1 x 4000 HC, 13 x 500 ANM64. Primary target: Dortmund. Weather 10/10ths cloud over target, tops 6/10,000 feet. Bombed at 16.57 hours from 19,000 feet on G.H. Leader.
12/03/1945	D	Lancaster III	ME529	A2-F	Dortmund	19,000	
					Bomb load 1 x 4000 HC, 12 x 500 ANM64. Primary target: Heinrichshutte, Hattingen Steel works & Benzol plant. Weather 10/10ths cloud, tops 7/12,000 feet. Bombed at 16.40 hours from 18,100 feet on leading G.H. aircraft.
14/03/1945	D	Lancaster I	PD389	A2-J	Heinrichshutte (Hattingen)	18,100	
					Bomb load 1 x 4000 HC, 13 x 500 ANM64, 2 x 500 MC. Primary target: Hamm Sachsen, Benzol plant. Weather 10/10ths cloud. Bombed at 14.02 hours at 18,400 feet on leading aircraft.
27/03/1945	D	Lancaster I	NN776	A2-D	Hamm Sachsen	18,400	
					Bomb load 1 x 4000 HC, 6 x 500 ANM64. Weather 10/10th cloud, tops 8000 feet. Bombed primary target Merseburg on centre of 3 Red flares & Green stars at 22.52 hours from 20,000 feet. Orange glow seen through the clouds. Arrived on time, no ground markings visible so we did in orbit until the skymarkers were placed. M.B. reception indistinct, bombing rather scattered.
04/04/1945	N	Lancaster III	ME529	A2-F	Merseburg (Leuna)	20,000	

Printed in Great Britain
by Amazon